Dan Kennedy, Bill Glazer, & Lee Milteer with the Peak Performers

Secrets of

Peak

Performers

Wealth Creating Strategies from the
World's Most Successful Entrepreneurs

V O L U M E   I I

Published by Advantage, Charleston, South Carolina.
Member of Advantage Media Group.

ADVANTAGE is a registered trademark and the Advantage colophon is a trademark of Advantage Media Group, Inc.

Printed in the United States of America.

ISBN: 978-1-59932-241-4
LCCN: 2010935618

This publication is designed to provide accurate and authoritative information in regard to the subject matter covered. It is sold with the understanding that the publisher is not engaged in rendering legal, accounting, or other professional services. If legal advice or other expert assistance is required, the services of a competent professional person should be sought.

Advantage Media Group is proud to be a part of the Tree Neutral™ program. Tree Neutral offsets the number of trees consumed in the production and printing of this book by taking proactive steps such as planting trees in direct proportion to the number of trees used to print books. To learn more about Tree Neutral, please visit www.treeneutral.com. To learn more about Advantage's commitment to being a responsible steward of the environment, please visit www.advantagefamily.com/green

Advantage Media Group is a leading publisher of business, motivation, and self-help authors. Do you have a manuscript or book idea that you would like to have considered for publication? Please visit www.amgbook.com or call 1.866.775.1696

CONTENTS

MONKEYS WITH TYPEWRITERS

DAN S. KENNEDY

IN THE NEWS THE WEEK I was writing this, a money manager-type was arrested, allegedly having stolen $30 million or so from his clients, including Hollywood celebrities like the money-mess Wesley Snipes. This, of course, is not a particularly rare news item. Hollywood celebrities, sports personalities, corporate CEO's and other wealthy people defrauded of their money by their managers, attorneys, investment advisors, Ponzi scheme operators, etc. is nothing new. In this case, as in most others, what would you wager that the clients just handed over their money and never checked the trading statements from third parties, examined or questioned investments, or got second opinions from uninvolved professionals? Did they read, study, and at least learn enough to ask smart questions? Of course not. Might as well stick a sign in your yard that says: *Everybody Away On Vacation. Big TV's And Jewelry Inside. Old, Toothless, Friendly Dog. Keys Under Mat.*

About the same time, I had an on-again, off-again client, with me for about 7 or 8 years, come for a consulting day with three people from his leadership team in tow. Late in the day, I gave the back-handed compliment that over years he had gone from flying blindfolded, by the seat of his pants to being much more in control of micro-numbers, statistics, facts, etc., to intelligently running his business – that, as much as his extraordinary marketing – being responsible for making him millions of dollars right now in a niche where many others are struggling.

He passes the responsible behavior test. The aggrieved actors looted for millions failed it. Where do you fall? Every day?

Every day, there is a test.

When you think about "peak performance," as this book asks you to do, where do you go first with your ponderings? Most people look for tactics and tools, technology or delegation, outsourcing, or magic beans of one kind or another: hypnosis, self-hypnosis, sub-liminal programming, meditation or visualization, or the latest color and number coded filing system, color-coded calendar, or electronic gizmo. But giving typewriters to monkeys has never produced a novel. Monkeys lack two things necessary to make productive use of the type-writers: knowledge and will.

For the sake of this conversation, we'll assume you possess some knowl-edge that has marketplace value and can be converted to income if pro-ductively applied. That leaves us with the will to do so.

That's the test. Will you? **This is *the* real deal.** *YOU* either get up in the morning, early, and *do it*, or you *don't*. Do or don't. That's how it is with everything – your health, your wealth, your book that may or may not get written, your commitments that may or may not be kept, your business' condition, your productivity and performance. You either *do it* or you *don't*. And the harsh reality is this: damn few people fail or suffer because of what they *can't* do. Because of what they *won't* and *don't* do. Not because of *can't*.

There are many, many ways to facilitate and support peak performance – of self, others or an organization. All worthy. But they are all typewriters in the hands of monkeys without will.

The diet book on the shelf, the treadmill in the basement, the marketing manuals at the office, the abundant opportunities at every turn – none have value without will.

Peak performance is a fundamental, philosophical, behavioral, intensely personal *choice*. It is inextricably linked with acceptance of *all* the responsibility for getting and achieving what you want. All of it. Without that choice made, without the will to honor it, any and all methodologies of peak performance are devalued. You can play with them, and play at appearing to be a peak performer, but that's all you're doing. Playing. Given typewriters, many monkeys *do* type. Or at least pound on the keys.

MYSTERIES THAT ARE ELEMENTARY, MY DEAR WATSON

We make many things – including peak performance – more mysterious than they are in order to mask our own very basic and fundamental failures of decision, determination and discipline.

I've been in the "success education" business for 35 years. I've seen, for example, incredibly complicated sales training "systems" come and go through corporate cultures. I've been selling my whole life. It isn't that complicated: get in front of high-probability prospects who can and will buy now (and avoid wasting time with anybody else), make a good and thorough presentation of a well-matched, appealing proposition, ask for the order, be resilient and persistent (because most yes' come after three no's), and, well, work. Sorry, but rocket science it isn't. Like

I always say about the famous sales trainer's 3-day boot camp where he teaches 365 closes – too bad he doesn't have *one* that works.

People who see my "fat photos" – when I carried 245 to 250 pounds – want to know my "secrets" for losing the weight and keeping it off. And most are bitterly disappointed with the answer. I eat a lot less crap, a lot less often. My diet and isometric exercise regimen are combined: sit in chair, place palms of hands against table's edge, and push your fat butt back until the food is out of reach. Very hard to sell that as a "system" in an infomercial.

Same deal with peak performance. It's not as mysterious as we'd like it to be. You get up. You have a day of productive, profitable things to do and you work – and fight not to have your work plan derailed. You really *work*. At night, you educate yourself so you can work smarter. Next day, repeat.

Oh, that education so you can work smarter thing, that's important. In fact, mastery of some specific, high value skill goes a long way.

WHAT ASSET IS BEST LEVERAGED BY PEAK PERFORMANCE?

One Sunday morning, while working in my cave, I took note of two things on the TV humming along across the room, and turned briefly to pay attention to both. They are both relevant here.

One was an infomercial for a juicer machine starring Jack LaLanne. He is 200 years old, looks great, and can still sell like the dickens. He's been telling his version of the Charles Atlas story and selling health stuff, like juicers, always in his trademark blue jump suit, longer than most people reading this have been out of diapers. And he's one of only three people ever to successfully sell juicers via infomercials, although many others have tried. It seems like such a simple thing to knock off. It looks deceptively easy, as many successes do. It occurred to me: isn't it interesting that they must use the *aged* fitness guru – that no new replacement of equivalent ability can be found? Montel Williams is in this game now and seems okay at it. But he's no Jack LaLanne. And here's what I'll wager about Montel, and about all others who have sought to sell such things: none of them have gotten their hands on *every* Jack LaLanne TV show, recording, and interview dating back to 1950. No one has watched them all, had them transcribed and thoroughly studied every gesture, facial expression, pause and the specific words he used. (For years people have been asking me how to become a really great platform sales speaker. When I tell them how, *no one* ever does it.)

The other show was a piece about the annual tournament for blind golfers. Yes. *Blind*. Each with a seeing eye dog and a coach, who puts the ball on the tee, lines up the shot, tells the golfer where and what, and they play – regular, real golf on a championship-tough golf course. The reigning champ, who has won 7 or 8 out of the past 10 years, hits a perfect drive over trees and lakes and drops it a few feet from the cup, better than Tiger (before he fell apart). With the strength of John Daly, but better accuracy. Then he putts that baby into the hole, first try. The guy is blind. As are the others competing. Tiger broke Gerald Ford's record and hit four, count'em four bystanders during the Memorial. This entire bunch of blind guys hit nobody.

Here's the message I take: *anybody* can absolutely, drop-dead master *any* damned thing they set out to master and attack with passion, intense study, determination, practice, and persistence. *Anybody* can master *anything*. Most people, of course, pass through this entire life without ever seriously attempting to master even one thing. Let alone actually doing so. And most people have a mile-long list of excuses for everything they can't do, can't do well, don't have time to do, and, not coincidentally, for the sorry state of their bank accounts, careers or businesses, and personal situations.

I don't see too many committed to mastery of anything, ever. I don't see many even willing to actually learn a lot about anything, just to be really well-versed in it. Less and less serious study, commitment or focus. Most peoples' knowledge is thinner than a slice of Arby's fake roast beef, but not wide either.

By the way, for the record, the blind guy who finished *last* would whip me silly on the golf course. Without his dog. And Jack LaLanne could kick my butt. But neither one can suck as much money out of the air with a pen as I can. So there.

Choice. Decision. Commitment.

Choice. Decision. Commitment. To mastery of some skill or skills, opportunity or opportunities that you can convert into all the money you could ever need, to get, to achieve and do all that you want.

Choice. Decision. Commitment. To apply those assets in the most productive way possible, every single day. To ace the test, daily. To refuse to let anybody screw it up for you.

THE WAR YOU ARE IN.
THE DAILY TEST.

In an interview during the campaign, then Senator Obama said that he imagined most Presidents only got to invest about 10% of their time in their agenda of choice, with 90% consumed by the agendas dictated by unforeseen circumstances. He may merely have been taking notice of a truth. Think Bush, 9-11, and all that it changed and demanded. Of far less importance but significant distraction, Clinton and the intern. Etc. Or, given his supreme arrogance, he might have been suggesting this was historically true of inferior mortals but would not affect him. As of this writing, he wrestles a Gulf oil spill, a worsening war, and the relationships with world leaders he promised to restore, now in the worst condition in decades – his agenda has been hijacked. His observation, though, is profound, and important to us all. Ultimately, how successful, rich, happy, etc. we are depends greatly on *what percentage* of our time stays safely connected to our own agendas, and *what percentage of it* we lose control of due to circumstances or other peoples' agendas, and *how often* we lose control to circumstances or other peoples' agendas. (These are MEASURABLE!)

This is *the* epic battle of life and the mundane battle of each day. Most people do not so clearly understand the war they are in. But I see everything through this frame. I know I face a global, local, familial and even internal conspiracy to rip my agenda from my paw and substitute another; one in which they have vested interests or of which they approve, while disapproving of mine. They are all waiting to wage this war, each and every morning. When I wake, they have already been readying themselves for the battle. I can sense them, just beyond the master-suite door. Smell their beastly breath.

Of course, there are mighty circumstances that rise up to threaten my agenda or yours or a President's. In a sense, Katrina's devastation and the Gulf spill were both preventable, had the government at these men's disposal been forced to do its proper preventive work, let alone respond properly. But to be fair, it's hard to hold any one person accountable for the oil spill, the hurricane, their aftermath, the outbreak of war or epidemic. In our own lives, illness or injury, assault on our rights or property by government or others, the simple nuisances of a four hour power failure or a blizzard blocking all the roads – these "circumstances" arrive with painful frequency, and certainly can substitute their agenda for yours or mine and, by the time they do arrive, there's damn little we can do but accept the new, imposed agenda for as brief a time as possible before returning to our own. Many of these circumstances are preventable: prevent time lost to power failures with a generator, prevent some illness with diet and supplements, prevent some injury by eschewing dangerous activity and being chauffered about in a tank. I have two idle computers so if one goes blooey, there's another waiting. Same with cars. But I do a dangerous thing 200+ times a year. This is a great puzzle: prevention. It is what apparently drove Howard Hughes into maximum seclusion – and madness. If you dedicate your life to prevention, that's its own agenda, isn't it?

But all these circumstances combined are less severe and constant and dominant of a threat to our agendas than our own behavior, and habits of behavior, with regard to the people we interact with, the access we give them, the influence on our thoughts and self-esteem and actions we permit them, the choices we make for ourselves – that most do not think of as choices at all.

That's the ultimate, core truth about this: peak performance is choice.

Will.

You will or you won't, you do or you don't.

Dan S. Kennedy is a multi-millionaire, serial entrepreneur; sought after marketing advisor and direct-response copywriter; speaker; and author of numerous books. His most recent books in the popular No B.S. series are *No B.S. Business Success In The New Economy, No B.S. Sales Success In The New Economy* and *No B.S. Wealth Attraction In The New Economy*, all available at amazon.com, BN.com, and all booksellers. Information @ www.NoBSBooks.com. His weekly political columns are published at BusinessAndMedia.org.

PEAK-A-BOO! YOU'RE LIKELY TO *HATE* THIS CHAPTER

BILL GLAZER

I'M HERE TO TELL YOU SOMETHING quite contrarian in this chapter about achieving Peak Performance and it's a good thing. Here it is….are you ready?

NO ONE EVER *"REALLY"* ACHIEVES PEAK PERFORMANCE.

Now I know this might sound strange to hear in a book about achieving Peak Performance, but I'm convinced it's true. It's your job to constantly improve your performance in order to move close to achieving Peak Performance, but no one actually ever achieves performance at a level that can't be improved on and made more efficient.

The reason why that's a good thing is because it makes all of "US" highly successful people always looking for ways to improve and this quest for constant improvement is what pushes us to always be better and better and better.

Okay, that was contrarian message #1 in my chapter (no one ever really achieves Peak Performance). Now let me drop contrarian message #2, the **W-Bomb** (not to be confused with the F-Bomb) on you. But before I do, some background information.

As a marketing strategist, for the past 30-years, I've worked with over 200+ of the most successful small business entrepreneurs in the world. I get to *peel-back-the curtain* with them and see first-hand what's going on in their businesses.

- The good

- The very good

- The bad

- The very bad

And

- The downright ugly.

Here's what I have observed are the three most common characteristics that the most successful entrepreneurs have in common:

1. They all have a constant thirst for additional knowledge and information. They realize that school is never out for the serious student and always invest in their education by reading relevant books, investing in resources, attending seminars, joining mastermind groups, and embracing the power of positive association.

2. They "all" put SYSTEMS in place so they can build a business based on doing it well once and then have it repeat over and over again. However, they understand that the "System" needs

to be constantly observed, tweaked, and tested for constant improvement.

3. They all…. (drum roll)….WORK. Yes, that's the W-Bomb I want to lay on you. The most successful entrepreneurs I know all embrace the concept of work and know that this is part of the game to be successful and to always move towards achieving more and more Peak Performance.

Two quick stories about this concept of "work" and they are both related to authors of books.

Story #1: When Tim Ferris released his best selling book, *The 4-Hour Workweek*, he was interviewed along with advertising strategist, Donny Deutsch on the *Today Show* by Matt Lauer. Matt first asked Tim questions about his book specific to his message of not having to work hard and achieve extraordinary success*. Then Lauer turned to Donny and asked him what he thought of this. Deutsch explained how he didn't buy into it at all. In fact, he went on to say that all of the successful entrepreneurs he knows and works with, actually have a passion for hard work and he thought they wouldn't be happy any other way.

Story #2: In Gary Vaynerchuk's best selling book, *Crush It!*, he makes an excellent point on page 88 when he refers to "hustle." He states that *"Someone with less passion and talent and poorer content can totally beat you if they're willing to **work** longer and harder than you are. Hustle is it. Without it, you should just pack up your toys and go home."* Throughout his book (which I highly recommend you read), Gary's pure message is to leverage your passion with the new online media to build your business and brand. But he is also astute enough to point out that without work you won't succeed.

17

Recently, when I was on a consulting phone call with a member of one of my "elite" Info-MASTERMIND Groups, I was presented with a question of how he can get 200 people into a multi-day seminar when he only has 300 customers and several thousand prospects. Plus, he only had a few months to accomplish this task.

Of course, he was looking for the "Easy Button" or said another way, "The Magic Pill."

I described to him a multi-step campaign which required:

- An immediate step to put into place to develop relationships with his prospects and further cultivate the relationship he has with customers

- A process to survey everyone to best match what he delivers with what they actually want

- A comprehensive marketing campaign involving multiple media including direct mail, email, webinars, teleseminars, and outbound telemarketing

- **AND…**a complete time frame to get everything accomplished, which meant he had to "hustle" and work his A _ _ off if he had a snowball's chance in hell to pull this off.

Of course, this conversation wasn't embraced with open arms. As I said before he was really looking for the 'Easy Button' and while at times you can get lucky and find one, you certainly can't count on it.

Now, before I end with my contrarian message about achieving Peak Performance, I do want to expand on this discussion about the W-Bomb. I don't want anyone to think that if they just work hard they will be super successful. The world is full with billions (that's billions with a "B") of people who work very hard just to get by and make a living.

Instead, what you have to do is work "smart." This now links back to the first two items on my list above. You have to have a constant thirst for additional knowledge and information and use that information to create repeatable "Systems" in place so that the work is done once and then you move onto creating the next "System."

In connection to all of this I mentioned that MASTERMIND Groups are an excellent source to acquire the knowledge and help that you need. Personally, I've been involved in the MASTERMIND process for over twenty years, both as a member and a facilitator. The only regret that I have about this is that I didn't embrace this sooner.

If MASTERMIND groups were appropriately named by the outcome they produce, you would really call them Shortcut Groups because that's what they really are. A shortcut to get the information you really need, from people you can rely on in the least amount of time.

In fact, I urge everyone reading this to join not one, but two MAS-TERMIND groups. One that is industry or occupation specific (i.e. information marketers, dentists, etc.) and one that is general category (successful people in all types of businesses you can tap into). You will find they both will bring you invaluable advice and shortcuts to getting closer and closer to Peak Performance.

To be fair to Tim Ferris, when we had him as a guest on one of our DIAMOND Tele-Coaching calls he made it clear that his book was not about not working hard. It is all about working smart.

Bill Glazer is a *Best Selling* author (**OUTRAGEOUS Advertising That's OUTRAGEOUSLY Successful**) and one of the most celebrated Marketing Strategists in the world. He is best known for his *OUTRAGEOULSY EFFECTIVE* direct-response advertising and direct mail. In fact, in 2002 Bill won the prestigious RAC Award. This honor is equivalent in advertising as the Oscars are to movies and the Emmys to television. In 2004 Bill teamed up with Marketing Guru, Dan Kennedy and they now provide marketing and business building advice to over 300,000 members and subscribers worldwide.

You can access "The Most Incredible FREE Gift Ever" containing over *$500.00 of Pure Money-Making Information* **courtesy of Dan Kennedy & Bill Glazer on page 134 of this book or at www.dankennedy.com**

BANISHING TIME AND ENERGY VAMPIRES FOR MORE PLEASURE AND PROFITS

LEE MILTEER

I AM REMINDING YOU that we only have 24 hours per day (no matter what a super hero you think you are) and our time is like a banking ledger—if you want to add something to one column, you have to subtract something from the other column; everything has to balance. One of the biggest challenges we have as entrepreneurs is to decide who and what gets our precious time allotments. Most busy entrepreneurs have a lot of commitments but no real plan or schedule for effectively organizing time, assessing where time is being lost, or evaluating time usage to see where adjustments need to be made. The bottom line is that most entrepreneurs and business owners have no "roadmap" for work days and frequently find themselves taking longer to accomplish things because items of importance are not appropriately prioritized in times or locations to make them more efficient.

Is your business running you or are you running it? Is your life steering you, or are you steering your life? These are important questions that you should think about and then do something about! You can accomplish greater things by making the most efficient use of your time if you create and follow a detailed schedule (more than just a "to do" list) for your work days. As an entrepreneur, it's important to take the time to PLAN and have the skill of awareness of where your time is going. Remember the oldest time management principle your teachers used to say: "Five minutes of preparation saves an hour of time." A planned schedule will decrease your effort, time spent, and frustration while increasing your mental health, physical health, and success in accomplishing your goals. Remember the old Proverb: "A good plan today is better than a perfect plan tomorrow."

Have you ever wondered how much more money or time off you could enjoy if you had better protocols for using your time? A very important question you should be asking yourself is: What non-productive time habits do I currently have that are robbing me of precious life energy—my time?

The truth is that you cannot chase tomorrow's opportunities with poor time skills. Most people allow short term pleasures such as email, surfing the web, mindless video games, silly TV shows, social media, friends, and bored associates to give them instant gratification. This is clearly counterproductive for innovation and success. I call these time wasters "mental delusions" because people confuse activity with productivity.

Most people are not conscious of how much time they waste and how much money they leave on the table every day from what I call Time and Energy Vampires. Most business owners don't have any systems or protocols to protect them. They react to life instead of acting in a way that allows them to use their time for profit work. Most time management systems were designed for people who have jobs and these one-size-fits-all systems simply do not work for entrepreneurs because we create our life with our blood, sweat, and tears. If you are not honoring yourself, you are out of integrity with your purpose for being self-employed.

In our current reality, we are programmed to believe that we have to be available 24/7. This isn't true and is actually bad business for you. In fact, you teach people how to treat you and what to expect from you. If you allow them to have access to you at all times, you are training them to expect that access at all times. The question you might ask yourself right now is: What am I teaching people to do concerning my time that is not serving me now or in the long run? This is a very important question because if you want to change your life and honor yourself more, you must start to be conscious of how you TEACH people to interact with you.

If you try to be all things to all people you are going to run yourself into the ground. To live a successful life, you must have boundaries that support your views and values. You must listen to your heart about what is right for you. It's not about what the world wants but what your individual needs are as an entrepreneur. If you give your personal power away to the outside world, someone will be happy to suck the marrow out of your bones. We have to take back our power. To be on top of our game, we must be in charge of our time.

Time is your most precious currency and as business people, we have the ability to replace money and business, but never time. The clock never stops moving, so remind yourself every day when you start your work that in your hourglass of today, there are only 1,440 minutes to utilize. 168 hours per week is your allotment to use your creative mind, talents, and physical hard work to manifest the business that supports the lifestyle that you want.

Part of being in integrity with your time is kicking the procrastination habit.

Stop putting profitable ventures on the back burner and start enacting today on important projects for new services, products, and even businesses.

There is no such thing as a perfect time and you have to decide today that you are going to stop talking about projects and actually get them started!

We all have great goals and one of the secrets of life is to start working on those goals. If you have great dreams and think that someday you will get started, please look on your calendar right now and schedule some dates. Unless you schedule it and make room in your life for these efforts, that "someday" is never going to happen. Think of it this way: Your time is linked to your integrity with self. Most people do not have true integrity with their time and therefore limit themselves in the amount of success, time off, and money in the bank. Please start to believe in yourself and give yourself permission to be brutally honest about where you are out of integrity with your time. Make a commitment that you are going to set aside time blocks and create boundaries with other people to work on your priorities instead of letting the vampires suck your most precious resource away from you—your time.

"He, who fails to plan, plans to fail."

—PROVERBS

Get Organized and Prevent Procrastination: Today is the day you can take back your life and learn to take advantage of small segments of time to get projects started that you have put off. Procrastinators are notorious for thinking they need a huge block of time to "really get started" on a project. Learn to use the 5-, 10- and 15-minute slots you find during the day to organize your materials, break down the project into steps, and begin to work on it. Once you start using small time slots, you will be amazed at how easy it will be to work on your project.

Don't think that the only time you've done well is when you've completed the entire project. If you wait to the end of projects to pat yourself on the back you will stay frustrated, which won't lead you to more creative thoughts, ideas, or money in your accounts.

Be realistic about time. Procrastinators tend to be poor time estimators and carry unrealistic expectations about what they can do in a given period of time. Estimate the time it takes to perform different tasks, then clock the reality of performing them. Give yourself enough time to reach your goals. If you have never done a time log, it would be a smart idea to "GET REAL" and do one to find out exactly what time it takes to do certain jobs.

Remind yourself of all of the negative consequences of procrastinating, including losing clients, customers, or patients. Think about the panic, guilt, self-criticism, and embarrassment associated with procrastination. How do you feel about the inferior work you couldn't review, or the late charges for past due payments?

Don't overbook yourself. Procrastinators tend to overload their schedules; they become angry with themselves when they can't get everything done. You aren't super human. You have a right to say "no" when unrealistic demands are made on your time. It is smart to schedule in some extra time because everything we do takes longer than originally thought.

Look at your schedule and build in 30 minutes a day to work on your dream projects.

Schedule and allow yourself free time. Long blocks of intense work aren't good for anyone. Be honest with yourself and identify your "best" work time; make good use of it. No one always works at peak capacity. You are the boss and you need to know when you do your best thinking and best productive work.

Learn to delegate responsibilities. Procrastinators often believe they should be able to do everything themselves. Since this is unrealistic, try identifying tasks of lesser importance and ask the best person to do them. One of the secrets of success is to only do what you are really good at and outsource or delegate the other work that is not profit work.

One of the top resources of all Peak Performers is that they take the time to play out the end result in their minds. Mentally rehearse or visualize how good you will feel when you finish the project. Let the positive vision help you get back on track. Remember, if you need a "procrastination break," take one. Just keep in mind that you are in control of it and it is not controlling you.

If you would like assistance and a clear road map to taking back your power come to my website: www.milteer.com and look under the products section for the Brand New Entrepreneur's Guide to Banishing Time and Energy Vampires System. I promise you this system is built for you as an entrepreneur and will bring you back into integrity with your life and purpose. Join Lee Milteer's Fellowship of Doers & Achievers Society!

INTEGRITY TO HONOR YOUR COMMITMENTS

Operate with Clear Goals and Targets: You must use a lot of information like goals, numbers, and statistics to help you hold yourself and the people you work with accountable if you want to be productive and profitable. You have to get out of being unclear and unfocused into the clarity of where your time and resources are really being spent. You have to be the one to set the deadlines for you and your staff. If you don't do this, no one will.

Work in a Productive Environment: I own my own office building where my staff works and where I have two personal working offices for me. One is for show for meetings, and the other, smaller office space is for serious creative planning work. However, all my writing and studying is done at my writing office at home. I block out time for planning, writing speeches and books, and all the creative work I need to do in my protected and quiet home space. I don't answer the door if the doorbell rings, I have caller ID, and I am in a very productive environment where I look out my window, see the beach, and feel good about myself. This allows me to honor my commitments easier because I have created a space that encourages me to write. I also have blocked the time I am in my home office and once I am there, I set a timer and I will not leave until that timer goes off, to remind me to take a small break. I have trained my brain to be creative and productive in that time and environment with clear targets to reach.

10 TIME MANAGEMENT CONCEPTS THAT HELP YOU PLAN AND EXECUTE YOUR OWN TIME SYSTEM FOR YOUR BUSINESS TYPE.

- *Avoid Activity Traps:* This is where you cannot see the forest for the trees. You get so wrapped up in what you are doing that you lose sight of why you are doing it.

- *Avoid Busyness:* Stop yourself and your staff from getting caught in activities and details surrounding an objective. Activity is not the same as productivity.

- *Be Aware of Murphy's Law:* Everything takes longer and costs more than you think it will. What can go wrong, will. Nothing is as easy as it appears.

- *You Must Plan:* You must determine what needs to be done, who and what gets it done, and by what time schedule.

- *You Must Have Priorities:* You must have a systematic arrangement of activities based on their order of importance.

- *Know the 80/20 Rule* (Pareto's Principle): It's proven that 80% of all results are derived from 20% of efforts.

- *Enact on Proactive Behavior:* You must not be reactive to situations in business but proactive by using positive movements toward the accomplishment of your goals.

- *Understand Effective vs. Efficient:* Get clear: effectiveness is doing the job right the first time. Efficiency is simply doing a job.

- *Scheduling:* Take the time to initiate planned activities and tasks that must be done.

- *Eliminate Timewasters:* Anything and Anyone who sidetracks you from the achievement of your goals.

In conclusion, I'd like to share some final words of wisdom. There is nothing, not burning desire or even money, more critical to personal and career success than the effective use of your time currency and your time integrity to self. I might also add that applying effective time management to your life will most likely be one of the biggest challenges you'll ever encounter as an entrepreneur. Until you have mastered your own boundaries, others will take your time and resources, so I highly recommend that you Join Lee Milteer's Fellowship of Doers & Achievers Society! Be proactive today and invest in a system that will guarantee you a new awareness of how to protect yourself and your time. My brand new system, The Entrepreneur's Guide to Banishing Time and Energy Vampires will supply you with the structure and protocols to map out your life in an entirely new and empowered direction. Go to www.milteer.com for resources. Your point of power is now, so be proactive about your most important asset—you!

Lee Milteer is a Performance Coach, Author, Professional Speaker, and TV and Radio Personality. She is the founder of the Millionaire Smarts® Coaching program. Lee has trained over a million people in her speeches. Her clients include Walt Disney, AT&T, XEROX, IBM, Ford Motor Co., NASA, Federal Express, plus hundreds of conventions.

Lee has shared the platform with Dr. Phil, Gene Simmons, Jack Canfield, Mark Victor Hansen, Tony Robbins, Zig Ziglar, Stephen Covey, Brian Tracy, Mike Ditka, Les Brown, George Foreman, and Joan Rivers to mention a few.

Lee has created educational programs airing on PBS and other cable networks plus video training for 350 of the top FORTUNE 500 companies and major universities, Bell Telephone, U.S. Navy, Dun & Bradstreet, U.S. Air Force and many private companies.

Lee is a recognized, best-selling book and video author. She is the author of the books: *Success Is An Inside Job, Spiritual Power Tools for Successful Selling* and CO-Author of *Walking with the Wise for Entrepreneurs, Reach Your Career Dreams, The Secrets of Peak Performers, The Phenomenon, Ultimate Entrepreneur Success Secrets,* and *Walking with The Wise Overcoming Obstacles.* Find out more at: www.milteer.com.

FREE BONUS: Visit www.milteer.com and download your free report: *Time Integrity for Entrepreneurs.* **Plus sign up for my FREE weekly** *Untamed Success* **e-newsletter that will empower you to be your authentic self and assist you to take control of your life and truly reach your potential.**

MARKETING YOUR WAY TO INDEPENDENCE:
SIMPLE & AFFORDABLE STRATEGIES FOR BUSINESS GROWTH IN THE DOWN ECONOMY

ADAM WITTY

DURING THE PANIC OF 1871 IN PARIS, everyone was selling. Everyone! Except for, of course, Baron Rothschild, who made a tidy fortune swimming against the tide and displaying confidence when everyone else was stricken with panic and paralyzed by fear.

And today, many entrepreneurs and small business owners are fighting tooth and nail to maintain their independence. The economic downturn that began in 2008 and continues now has left many businesses bruised, battered, and broken. In fact, most business owners have a hard time remembering economic times as brutal as those we are currently experiencing.

The disastrous market conditions of the past 18 months have provided a parallel to the panic of 1871—and some incredible deals, if you are daring, creative and entrepreneurial enough to see them. During these troubled times, it's important for business owners to behave like the late great Baron Rothschild and look for the opportunity amidst the rubble (a key secret to being a Peak Performer)!

It is possible to prosper and grow your business in a down economy. In fact, there is no better time to do it. With the large majority of companies cutting back and dramatically decreasing their investments in marketing, now has never been a better or more affordable time to market.

From one entrepreneur to another, let me share with you four simple marketing ideas to maintain and grow your business. These are marketing campaigns my company, Advantage Media Group, is currently running. Before you say "but my business is different," let me say "no it isn't." If these tactics can work for Advantage, they can work for you. You simply need the creativity to apply these ideas to your own business.

Let's get started.

1.) LAUNCH A CUSTOMER GET A CUSTOMER CONTEST

Earlier this year, after a review of Advantage's 2009 marketing efforts, I learned that despite investing tens of thousands of dollars into marketing and advertising, 67% of Advantage's new authors came from introductions from existing authors, friends, and associates. The "smack my forehead" moment came when I realized we were investing far more money into getting 33% of our new authors (non referrals) than we were investing to get 67% of our new authors (from referrals). I would rather spend money on my authors than on buying advertising.

So here is what we did. We launched **Author Get An Author** (www. AuthorGetAnAuthor.com). Every time an individual makes a quality introduction, we place that person's name on a ping pong ball and throw it in a hopper.

At the end of the year, we are going to have a live drawing and pull one of the ping pong balls out of the hopper. One of our authors is going to win the Grand Prize and receive a FREE two-week vacation to the Mediterranean, **or** two tickets to the Super Bowl, **or** 5,000 copies of their book. They choose.

To really get people excited, we mail a hand written thank you note after every introduction. In addition, we include a praline cookie and a flyer that includes a live update of the number of ping pong balls they have in the hopper. To increase their chances of winning, all they have to do is make more quality introductions.

2.) OFFER FREE TO INDUCE A PURCHASE

Last fall, we officially launched Advantage Television (www.Advantage.tv). To induce our clients to hire us to produce a regular internet television show for them and their business, we decided to offer a free sample. No different than the girls on the streets of Charleston offering a free sample of Italian ice as a ploy to get you hooked, we did the same thing. We offered the 1st 10 authors to respond 1 free custom television show. They have to travel to Charleston to tape. We are confident that once they see how great their show looks, they will want to purchase a 12 month package.

3.) LISTEN TO YOUR CUSTOMERS AND HOST A CUSTOMER APPRECIATION DAY

In October, Advantage will host its annual Author Marketing Summit (www.AuthorMarketingSummit.com).

After listening to author feedback, we found the most common question we get is related to starting and building a professional speaking business. To meet the needs of our customers, we decided to offer a 100% FREE bonus day to our conference titled: A-Z Blueprint: Building a Profitable Speaking Business. By offering our authors exactly what they want, we have been able to increase enrollment to our conference dramatically.

4.) CONNECT YOUR BUSINESS WITH CHARITABLE CAUSES

Advantage Media Group celebrated its five year anniversary in July of 2010. Rather than throwing a party and blowing money on cake, decorations, and food...we thought it would be far more constructive, meaningful, and exciting to use that money and energy to do something for others.

Advantage launched an ambitious 30 day campaign to raise the money to construct a library in a third world country for underserved children. Here is how we structured the deal:

Advantage partnered with Pencils of Promise (pencilsofpromise.org), a 501(c) 3, a leader in coordinating the building of libraries and schools for impoverished children in third world countries.

Laos is one of the poorest Asian countries in the world. Most children have no access to education whatsoever.

It costs $5,000 US dollars to build and furnish a school library in Laos. Advantage contributed the first $1,000, and then asked our authors, partners, and friends to contribute the additional $4,000 needed to get the job done.

Donations go directly to Pencils of Promise and are 100% tax deductible. Advantage was simply coordinating the effort.

Everyone that contributed will have their name engraved on a plaque permanently placed inside the library. Furthermore, a copy of their book will be placed on the library shelves for the children of Laos to read.

The library we built will serve high school students who are all eager to learn English.

By connecting with your customers on a more altruistic level, it will allow you to build bonds and connection points that transcend simple commercial transactions. Your job is to weave your business into your customer's lives. Partnering with a charity and inviting your customers to participate is an excellent way to do this.

In closing, I would simply remind you that we live in a tough business world. As an entrepreneur, you must out-hustle and out-work your competition. Furthermore, you must be different, and constantly be doing different things. The definition of insanity is doing the same thing over and over yet expecting a different result. Take any four of the ideas above, customize them to your business, and prepare to see your business grow. Please be sure to report back to me the results. Happy marketing!

ADAM WITTY is the Founder and Chief Executive Officer of Advantage, heading up strategic business development and growth opportunities for the company. What began in the spare bedroom of his home is now an international media company with leading businesses in book publishing, magazine publishing, and television & video.

Adam is the author of *21 Ways to Build Your Business with a Book*, *21 Ways to Build Your Business with a Magazine* and co-author of *How To Build Your Dental Practice With a Book*, *How to Build Your Law Practice with a Book* and *Click: The Ultimate Guide to Internet Marketing for Authors*. Adam's weekly television show *Author Advantage TV*™ and *Entrepreneurs Library TV*™ can be seen on internet television station Advantage.tv. In addition, Adam serves as the Publisher of *Author Advantage Magazine*™ and president of the Author Marketing Summit™.

Adam is an in-demand speaker, teacher, and consultant on marketing and business development techniques for entrepreneurs and authors and is a frequent guest on the acclaimed Extreme Entrepreneurship Tour. Adam has been featured in *Investors Business Daily*, *Young Money Magazine*, and on ABC and Fox.

Adam serves on the Board of Directors of Advantage Financial Partners, a Peruvian based micro finance bank; Youth Entrepreneurship South Carolina (YEScarolina); and the Charitable Society of Charleston. Adam is a proud alumnus of Clemson University and happy to call Charleston home.

SPECIAL GIFT TO READERS: Do you have a manuscript or book idea that you would like considered for publishing? Visit www.AMGBook.com, complete our Publishing Questionnaire, and receive a complimentary 30-minute book consultation.

Do you have an idea for a internet television show or a custom video project? Visit www.Advantage.tv, complete our TV & Video Questionnaire, and receive a complimentary 30-minute television and video consultation.

STAR-STUDDED STEPS TO BUILDING A SUCCESSFUL SOCIAL MEDIA MARKETING SYSTEM

DIANE CONKLIN & GAIL SASEEN

SOCIAL MEDIA "MARKETING" is one of today's biggest trends. Everyone is in on it, or wants to be. For some, it's a daunting task of learning new acronyms, marketing rules, and determining the time expenditure. The truth of the matter is, if you have a business—retail, online, or brick and mortar, you really need to become comfortable with Social Media.

Once you decide to jump in, you'll probably want some help getting started. There are many so-called experts now jumping on the band wagon. Be careful as you begin to put resources behind Social Media.

Below are 8 simple steps you can take to get off to a good start, FAST.

STEP 1 ~ GET SMART

There are three reasons why you might not be taking advantage of the seemingly unlimited power of Social Media in their marketing strategies:

First, is simply because you've never taken the time to understand it.

Social Media Lead Generation System

Educate Yourself
- Learn What You Need To Know
- Hire an Expert to do everything for you?
- Understand the Basics
- What does your market want
- Can You Provide That Information To Them
- Where does your target market congregate

Define Your Goals
- Promote Your Products & Services
- Promote Yourself as an Authority
- Drive Targeted Leads To your Website

Identify The Media You Want To Participate in
- Facebook
- Twitter
- Squidoo
- LinkedIn
- Your Own Blog
- Article Marketing
- Other

Define Your Strategy
- How Do You Want To Communicate and Present Yourself?
- Are you promoting yourself?
- How will you promote your product or service?
- How does Social Media fit into your overall marketing strategy?
- How will you brand yourself?
- What is

What Is Your Time Commitment
- Hours Per Day?
- Days Per Week?
- Schedule?

Define Your Budget
- Cost of Your Time
- Cost of Assistance

How Will Your Measure Your Success
- Leads or Optins per week
- Leads or Optins per Month
- Sales from Social Media Leads
- Other??

Build Your System Technology
- Done For You
- You Do It
- Build a WordPress Blog
- Squeeze Page / Optin
  - Give Away?
  - Low Cost Intro Product?
  - Teleseminar?
- Thank You page with One Time Offer
- Autoresponder — Build Your Autoresponder Messages
- Product Download Page
- Audio - Video
- Product Creation
- Sales Page
- Write your promotional messages

Next, is because you think social media marketing will take too long to learn and implement.

Finally, you don't think you have the technical expertise to implement it.

Tip: *Use the K.I.S.S. principle (Keep It Simple Stupid). Concentrate on the basics.*

What I hear most often from my friends, associates and business partners is, most business owners think learning Social Media is overwhelming, what are the short cuts, are there any "Cliff Notes"? (Remember those little yellow and black cheat books we used in high school and college so we didn't have to read the entire book?)

You must at least get a "Cliff Notes" understanding of Social Media and how it works, even if you hire a professional. As the business owner, you must provide content to the technician who is building and implementing your system. You should also research your market and get a feeling of what they are looking for and talking about.

STEP 2 ~ GET CLEAR BEFORE YOU START

As with every type of media integrated into your marketing plan, you really must determine *your* "why" as you implement Social Media marketing in your business. It's much easier to work backwards from the goal than to "wing" it. Working backwards from your goal will help you keep your eye on the goal and on track. That's called getting "clear."

Social Media marketing can be used to do many things, such as:

•   Drive traffic to your website,

•   Build brand awareness,

- Generate referrals or

- Simply open lines of communication with your customers and prospects.

Tip: Decide what you want to accomplish before you start.

Some people jump into Social Media with the goal of accumulating as many "friends" and followers as possible. That's **_OK,_** BUT…, wouldn't you rather have a list of thousands who were _interested_ in you and your product and service? Wouldn't you prefer to have your friends list "targeted" to the type of customer or client you would love to have?

Big numbers of friends and followers are great, but if they aren't "interested" in your niche, they certainly will not become loyal customers.

There is no question that attracting thousands of friends and followers can definitely help your business grow. Attracting friends and followers is one thing, keeping them and then converting them to actual customers is a completely different matter.

The quickest way to be banished and ignored in any network is to blatantly "sell them." Rather than presenting offer after offer, you should provide great content and information, ideas and suggestions that your friends, fans and followers will find useful. How you accomplish this challenge is part of your overall Social Media strategy.

Once you define your specific measurable business goals for participating in social media networks your next steps will be much easier and you will become more focused.

STEP 3 ~ IDENTIFY SOCIAL MEDIA NETWORKS TO START WITH

There are literally thousands of Social Media platforms you could use in your marketing strategy. This is why you, like some other business owners don't incorporate social media. You simply don't know which Social Media networks to join. You might be so unsure that they procrastinate or do nothing.

Here is a simple philosophy that should make sense to you.

Tip: Start with the most popular social media networks being used by the most people.

The choice becomes obvious! Today, these include YouTube, Facebook, Twitter and LinkedIn. Once you get yourself established with those, you can think about adding Social Bookmarking, blogging strategies and more. That's how you narrowed down the thousands into a manageable handful that will cover most of what you need.

STEP 4 ~ DEVELOP YOUR WINNING STRATEGY

If you're like most, you expect the most results in the least amount of time. You also want your return on your investment to be high, right?

As you develop your Social Media marketing strategy, you should consider:

- How does Social Media fit into your overall marketing plan?

- What other marketing medias are you using to support your Social Media efforts (direct mail, postcards, telephones, voice broadcasts, freebies and giveaways)?

- How do you promote your brand?

- How will you introduce your products and services?

The question is, do you want to start from scratch and learn all of this "stuff" on your own? You might want to right now, but isn't your time in your business not better spent elsewhere? How long will it take you to learn? Isn't time an issue for you like it is for most entrepreneurs? How valuable is your time?

> *Tip: Automate what you can, eliminate what you don't need, DELEGATE most everything else.*

If you truly want speed, which means saving time and money, hire someone qualified to do it for you. You develop the content and strategy and let the experts build the system for you.

STEP 5 ~ HOW MUCH TIME CAN YOU SPEND

Time is money, right? Many of the folks I've spoken to who object to getting involved in social networking have these common objections: "I don't have the time to do that! I'm too busy!' It's addicting!" Sound familiar?

While some entrepreneurs are doing all of their own tweets and posts, many have hired an expert to do the actual tweeting and blogging for them. You can do that as well.

Let's face it; we all make time for the things in our life and business that are important to us. You don't need to spend as much personal time as you think. Here are the keys….

- Set a schedule – twice a day for no more than 20 minutes each time.

- Re-purpose your existing content or have your assistant do it for you.

- If you value your time, you can make Social Media work for you by setting boundaries and sticking to it or delegating the lion's share of the work.

Tip: Set a timer to keep yourself in integrity.

There are a litany of tools that can "kill 2 birds with 1 stone", per say. Tools such as, Tweetdeck, HootSuite, ping.fm and many more can help you write a post once and simultaneously post to several networks. You can also do a search for Twitter Tools and you'll see there are 100's of tools.

STEP 6 ~ WHAT IS YOUR BUDGET

The best part about Social Media is that most, if not all, the websites that you'll use are free. Twitter, Facebook and YouTube for instance are all free. Those are three of the websites you'll most likely be using.

On the other hand, some websites like LinkedIn offer premium services for a nominal charge. Once you decide how you are going to use each site, you can decide whether to upgrade or not.

Tip: Determine your hourly rate. Then decide whether or not you should outsource.

Most of the money you'll spend on Social Media marketing will be in the form of time – either your own, a staff member or an outside consultant or expert. If you decide to hire an assistant to handle specific parts of your Social Media efforts, be sure to allocate the appropriate funds to do so.

STEP 7 ~ HOW WILL YOU MEASURE YOUR SUCCESS

You should consider several elements when you measure your Social Media marketing success. Customize how you calculate your **Return On Investment (ROI)** by factoring in:

- How many leads per day

- How many leads per week

- How many leads per month

- How many new leads per campaign or launch

- How many sales

- Dollar value of the sales

Set up a simple spreadsheet and calculate daily, weekly or whatever you deem appropriate for your business. Just be sure that measurement becomes routine. You might be surprised at the trends that develop. Once you identify the trends, you can adjust your strategy to increase your ROI.

Tip: Grab a complimentary measurement tool at:
www.socialmedialeadssystem.com/tools.html

Are other people talking about you or your company? Are they "re-tweeting" your tweets, attending your events and joining your groups?

Are you engaged in conversations, what you do and how you can solve their problems? All of these things eventually lead to increased sales.

Social Media should lead to new clients and increased sales and profits.

Having those back links to your website from Social Media websites like Facebook and YouTube can have a significant impact on Google organic search results.

Your Social Media marketing strategy should be treated like all of your other marketing efforts – either do it right or don't do it all.

STEP 8 ~ BUILD YOUR TECHNOLOGY – IMPLEMENT

This step is where many fall short. **Implementation!**

You start doubting yourself and allow the fear of something unknown to stop you dead in you tracks. Another element that slows implementation is procrastination. You know…. "Oh, well – I'll start on this next week." It's human nature. We all tend to put off things that are uncomfortable, new or things we don't understand.

Tip: Nothing happens unless you take action!

The best plan of attack is to hire an expert to put the pieces together and teach you how to continue on once your system is built.

If you'd like to receive simple and easy information about implementing Social Media in your business, visit http://www.SocialNetworkLeads-System.com and receive an immediate download of our FREE EBook Titled, "How to Get Social Media Working IN Your Business Today, 8 Simple Steps to Building A Successful Social Media System".

Diane Conklin & Gail Saseen are internationally known marketing and business strategists. They are also authors, entrepreneurs, marketing coaches, consultants, event planners, speakers, direct mail experts, and copywriters. Having over 24 years of combined experience in the Information Marketing business, they have earned their reputation as implementers - that means they know how to get things done!

Diane specializes in showing small business owners, entrepreneurs, coaches and consultants how to integrate their marketing strategies, media and methods to get maximum results from their marketing dollars. Diane is also an Event Planning and Marketing expert. She planned and produced events grossing over $1,000,000.00. She has also participated in Direct Mail campaigns that have grossed over $1,000,000.00 in sales.

Gail specializes in helping entrepreneurs turn their knowledge into profits through the power of Information Marketing. She excels in coaching and consulting with entrepreneurs and small business owners to help solve their business challenges relating to Social Media integration and website technology, marketing strategies, product development, affiliate programs, lead generation, and list management.

Through their company, **Complete Marketing Systems, LLC.**, Gail and Diane offer a wide range of programs and services for start-up business, both online and offline, all the way up to well established businesses.

Diane and Gail have social media programs that show you how to make real money with Social Media in 27 minutes or less a day and they also provide Social Media Management services for those who want the benefits of social media but don't want to do it themselves. For more information call (866) 293-0589 or for a copy of their free book *How To Get Social Media Working In Your Business Today* go to www. SocialNetworkLeadsSystem.com.

THE PSYCHOLOGY OF FOLLOW UP...
HOW TO USE E-MAIL MARKETING
2.0 TO DOUBLE YOUR SALES

COLIN DAYMUDE

IT'S COMMON WISDOM amongst regular folk and guru's alike that one of the key factors in success in life is the ability to delay immediate gratification. In fact, Stanford University conducted a study a few years ago that backed up that very premise. The researchers put a group of kids in a room and found a direct correlation between their ability to delay immediate gratification and success. The kids were offered one marshmallow right away or two marshmallows in 15 minutes after the researchers returned to the room. The math is obvious; a 100% return on *sweet* equity. As impressive as that is, it's not just the initial return that raised my eyebrows. The two-marshmallow kids were in the distinct minority meaning that *most* people cannot delay immediate gratification even for a short period of time. But the two-marshmallow group also had much better social relations and scored an average of 210 points higher on their SAT scores.

Now think about your business and your sales process. Most people and companies are looking for the quick return. Even public companies only think a quarter ahead and their sales team (the vast majority of them) are going for the one marshmallow every day; the quick sale, regardless of the needs of the company or the client. And if the sale can't be made quickly then it's move on to the next prospect. Absolutely no regard for the customers who might not be ready to buy now and absolutely no regard for the customers who are not a good fit for the product. Sell at all cost and sell now. And the price is all the converted leads who were not a good fit (who then become raving complaints) and the high percentage of unconverted leads which were a good fit (who could have become raving fans).

Now, imagine your potential life mate, husband or wife. You see them in a restaurant from across the room. You *know* that they are the *one*. So what's your next move? Well, if you are a one marshmallow person then you simply walk up and propose marriage. Yeah that sounds completely crazy but it's interesting that that is exactly what the vast majority of sales people do. No research, no segmentation based on behaviors, buying patterns, needs etc. Finding the ideal lifelong mate or your ideal customer is the *same* process. It starts with initial infatuation and from there it's a discovery process. Get the facts out on the table and make sure it's a good fit. If it is, then there is no *selling* involved. The pieces of the puzzle just go together seamlessly.

Just last month I presided over InfusionCon as the Master of Ceremonies (M.C.). InfusionCon is the free annual Conference for Infusionsoft users. It was an amazing event of close to 1000 entrepreneurs who are bucking the trend of the Great Recession and producing stellar results in sales and profits. Infusionsoft users are true two-marshmallow people. They use an amazing piece of software that combines Customer Relationship Management, E-commerce and Email Marketing all in one automated application to do the discovery process for them, *automatically*. It compiles details about what people are interested in, what their buying habits, wants and desires are and then intuitively talks to them according to the same. In other words, the software actually forms and maintains a relationship with customers. That's what

Email Marketing 2.0 is. Messages are relevant so people are interested in them; the emails get opened and people *buy*. The bottom line is that all businesses need an automated system that is scalable and sends relevant information to the right people, at the right time, using the right media (email, video, hard copy, text). That's why hundreds of Infusionsoft customers doubled their sales in 2009 alone, in *this* economy.

Imagine this; you hire a copywriter to write a great letter and you send it out to a list of 5,000 addresses that you have compiled and you drive them all to a website. It doesn't matter how this story starts (how your leads are generated) but what happens after that is one of the greatest opportunities in business today. What if each of those 5000 people got the exact same quality education about your product? But not just quality, but targeted education based on what the customer was actually looking for? And that education helped your potential customer gain familiarity with you and the product; familiarity to the point that enough trust and understanding builds up and few barriers exist for them to buy? And all of the people who were interested in your widget were captured based on their individual wants and needs and communicated to accordingly (some people *like* product A and some people *like* product B)? And what if your conversion rate for purchase was 95% higher because of the relevancy of the information? And what if, after the purchase, systems were in place that constantly educated your new customers about their purchase and re-sold them so buyer's remorse was at the lowest point possible? And what if, because of all of that, your new customers became raving fans and told thousands of other customers about your amazing service and products?

And when those referrals came in, you wouldn't need additional staff because your systems are scalable and working whether you are or you are not? That all happens when your system is automated.

And what about all of the customers who didn't buy initially? Well unless your business is a complete anomaly then it is like every other business; the vast majority of leads *don't buy*. But given the chance over time, many of those customers may want the opportunity to buy after the initial offer. The reasons that people don't buy initially can vary widely. No money, not enough interest, interest in other products, pre-purchase remorse and the list could go on and on and on. But frankly it doesn't matter all that much. What matters is that you continue to maintain a relationship until they either opt out of your marketing or buy from you.

And now imagine your world without systems in place when that initial letter is sent out (you remember, the 5000 piece mailer). It's the world that *most businesses live in* and the reason that most of them fail. In this scenario, you do everything manually, using numerous cumbersome systems. If the right prospect gets the right information, using the right media, at the right time, it will not be due to the great systems you have in place, it will be due to pure luck. And if you do get "lucky" and people actually do buy, what about everything that happens next?

Fixing your follow up failure is nothing new. In fact "follow up failure" starts when we are kids and escalates in puberty with sweaty palms and a fear of calling the girl back after the first fateful encounter. And for the girl who never gets the phone call, follow up failure becomes a rite of passage.

In all seriousness though, follow up failure occurs in business for a variety of reasons. All valid and all capable of turning your business into the wrong kind of statistic. Sometimes we don't follow up because of a fear of failure, sometimes because of a fear of success (what if a big potential client *does* say yes and we have to fulfill?), most of the times because we just have too much to do and not enough of "us" to do it. But regardless of the reasons, what is important is that you recognize the lost opportunities in your business and fix your follow up failure.

Its been said that if you want to be successful, then find out what everyone else is doing and then do just the opposite. Well here's a good picture about what everyone else is doing; statistics show that most sales (a full 81%) are made on the fifth customer contact with a customer. In fact just 2% of sales are made on the first contact and just 3% are made on the second contact.

But what's most important about those statistics is that most people just give up too soon. They are not in it for two marshmallows. It's either one now or one later. Studies also show that 90% of businesses *stop* following up before the critical fifth customer contact. 48% actually quit after the *first* contact.

So it's easy to see just how to differentiate your business from most every other business in your channel. Just fix your follow up failure, all the way through the sales cycle, pass go and collect your two marshmallows.

Colin Daymude is an entrepreneur, national speaker, trainer, coach and author of two books and numerous industry white papers, Colin founded The Annual Mortgage Marketing Review Conference and was former CEO of the fastest growing training company in the US. Colin has personally and/or through Infusionsoft consulted with thousands of businesses and has been described as being on the "cutting edge as a speaker and marketing expert."

Currently Colin coordinates partner relationships for Infusionsoft and as the CEO of CCCS Marketing, he understands entrepreneurs from the ground floor. If you have an event or a company function and you need a dynamic, creative keynote speaker then please contact him for availability.

Please take advantage of my offer to get a free report on Email Marketing 2.0. You can take advantage of this opportunity at www.infusionsoft.com/peak. And for information about partnering with Infusionsoft or to inquire about having Colin speak at one of your events please inquire at www.infusionsoft.com/partner-programs.

BETTER RESULTS. BETTER BUSINESS. BETTER LIFE.

LEARN HOW TO FINALLY BE ABLE TO DO BUSINESS ON YOUR OWN TERMS!

BOB HOLDSWORTH

IS YOUR BUSINESS STUCK? Worse, are you stuck in your business?

Are you working more, getting less and feeling like your business is sucking the life out of you?

Do you want to finally be able to, *Do business on your own terms!*[*] You can. It's never to late to RESET your life or your business and have success on your own terms.

Results are inevitable. The difference between Peak Performers, [the top 11% of highly successful entrepreneurs] and the remaining 89%, is that Peak Performers share the steel-willed determination, focus and endurance that it takes to shape and influence the results that **THEY** want and they develop the ability to get them on their own terms.

By Webster's definition, a result is:

"something that comes out of or follows from an activity or process..."

If I take liberty with that definition; creating positive, life changing results is the direct result of a personally created, well designed, sequentially implemented, action *process*'.

As a marketing and business growth coach, most of my work time is spent with other entrepreneurs. To date, I've had the good fortune to have worked with business owners in 48 different industries. I still find it fascinating that, regardless of industry, every business owner wants the same basic three results

Result #1: A lucrative business

Result #2: More time with family

Result #3: A superior lifestyle

What I've also discovered is that every one of these very smart, hard working and motivated individuals readily admits that at least one of these areas of their life is out of whack and they don't know how to fix it. In a word, they're ***stuck***.

The key to getting un-stuck and unlocking your success can be found in six simple words that every business owner has *heard* time and time again. Although 100% of them have *heard* the words, the statistics repeatedly show that few actually commit to taking the sustained actions required by the words.

Here they are… the six words that can change your business, family and lifestyle… "*Dream It…Design It…DO IT!*" They seem simple enough, but they're not.

All of us can dream about what we want, in fact dreaming can eat up days, weeks and even years of our lives. Designing it, re-designing it and re-designing it again can eat up still more days, weeks and years. The hardest part, the one that paralyzes most people in fear, and thus becomes their point of failure, is the '*DO IT*' part.

The vast majority of people are derailed by second guessing. What if it doesn't work? What if people I trust challenge my hopes and dreams? What if I actually take a step, start doing something only to have it crash and fail? Maybe I should go slower and change the dreams, re-design a safer dream or maybe I should just wait, because now might not be the right time?

If you've already started your business and things aren't going well either in your business or your personal life, don't worry you can start over, not literally…I call the process '*Hitting the RESET Button*'. I'll talk a lot more about the process shortly.

Don't get sucked in or disabled by these or any other excuses, go out there and "*Dream It, Design It and DO IT!*" I've created a great video on implementation and how to avoid the 11 most common things that derail people. Go to **www.BobHoldsworth.com** and sign up for the FREE video series…the first of the four free videos is on implementation.

For those of you who actually want to read and write rather than watch, I've also created something that will help you. My *Success Factors Wealth Building System*ˢᵐ is a systematized process that will help guide your thoughts and show you how to apply three basic building blocks to any area of your life that you want to improve. By following the process, I assure you that you will get un-stuck and that significant positive results and increased 'wealth' in your life and your business will follow.

At the end of this chapter you'll find a link to a FREE online e-workbook that I've created just for the readers of this book that will help you get started.

Here's a very short overview explaining the core principles of the powerful, life changing, *Success Factors Wealth Building System*ˢᵐ.

BUILDING BLOCK #1 — **DREAM IT**

You can do this process in each area of your life that you want to improve. We all have to start somewhere so pick the one area of your life that you most want to improve first. Select the statement that best describes your current situation:

- Business is great, but there's no personal or family time.

- I've got lots of personal time because business stinks.

- Business is good and there's time for family, but I'm not living my dream life yet.

After choosing your area of focus, start by writing down every dream related to that part of your life. When I ask clients if they've ever done this, most say no, they have no time. My question is how will you ever be 'successful' and 'happy' if you don't truly know what you want? It's ok to be a little self-centered here and to think big…it's your life, what do you *really* want from it?

If you are feeling stuck in the business or the life that you've created and you've identified the most important thing that you really want to change, it's time to complete the next phase of the *Success Factors Wealth Building System* and then it will be time to actually get up the nerve to '*hit the RESET button*' and to take action.

Once you are officially 'dreamed out' go back through your list, prioritize what you've written and then move to Building Block #2.

BUILDING BLOCK #2 — **DESIGN IT**

Start with your most important dream and design a plan to achieve it. By writing, thinking and getting focused help from your subconscious mind, you'll discover new options that will finally allow you to begin to achieve your dreams.

If you don't take the time to design your way around, over, or through the obstacles standing between you and your dreams, you'll never get there.

Will you need to learn new skills? Will you need to invest in technology? Who do you know that's successful doing what it is that you want to do? Make an appointment and take that person to lunch to discover how they manifest the results you want. Contrary to popular belief, most successful people are very approachable and are willing to give back by helping others achieve success.

Again, don't hold back. You are designing your dream life here...what's supposed to be in it? More importantly, if you're already stuck, what's NOT supposed to be in it?

BUILDING BLOCK #3 — **DO IT**

Now comes the moment of truth, the take action, the DO IT part. It's time to take your dream and your design plan and put them together into a definitive written timetable...with dates, times, people, resources, and most of all your intended results!

I know it can seem impossible at first but you can do it. Start small if you have to, but *start!*

> *Visit our YouTube Channel for a great free video on setting*
> *SMART goals: www.YouTube.com/BobHoldsworthGroup*

If you're just starting out, this information will get you thinking and get you on the right path. If you need to '*hit the RESET button*' let me briefly describe how that happens. You've identified your dream, written your goals, you've designed the desired results. Now, as part of the *DO IT* stage, you need to pick a date and a time to start. Symbolically '*hitting the RESET button*' and from that moment on, what came before is in the past. I hit the button on April 25, 2005 after redesigning my life at 46 and deciding how I'd live my second half.

I invite you to read how I created 'Boys Day', turned my personal slogan into a registered trademark, and why that date in April was such a turning point for me and my family.

My personal success story is at **www.BobHoldsworth.com/story**

You might think that I'm spouting some sort of pie-in-the-sky wishful thinking. I can assure you I'm not. If the dreams that you write down are truly important to you, and you really want to join the 11% who 'get it', then you will find a way to make them happen and the symbolism of '*hitting the RESET button*' on a specific date and time becomes very real for people who are serious.

No excuses. No immovable obstacles. No quitting. This is **your** life, **your** family and **your** business…take control, create and define the success you want in your life and ***Do business on your own terms!*** *

Start today. Start now. You CAN do this!

BOB HOLDSWORTH has a crazy and diverse work history beginning with a stint as a student news broadcaster, part-time TV cameraman and on-air disc jockey in college. After that came positions as unit managers for three large national food service corporations, 4 ½ years in prison...as a corrections officer and a medic working in a maximum security facility, 25 years as a paramedic and over 20 years as a successful entrepreneur.

Bob owns and operates two successful professional service businesses, a multi-million dollar medical billing company he founded in 1988 that commands a 31% market share in its home state, and maintains a 93% client retention rate. His second, The Holdsworth Group, is a rapidly growing marketing and business growth coaching practice.

As a coach/consultant, the diversity in his background helps Bob bring new ideas and fresh thinking to his client engagements. His work has touched more than 810 organizations from 48 different industries that range from a one person massage therapy practice, numerous small to mid-sized companies, to the US Navy, and Fortune 100 and 500 companies.

He's worked with them in the areas of strategic business planning, executive coaching, new product development, entrepreneurship, ROI-based marketing effectiveness, leadership, teambuilding, putting family first and the profitable process of turning new customers into long term clients.

Bob is a sought after speaker, a nationally published author, a happily married husband and the dad of two awesome twin boys. He's a dangerously bad golfer, an avid reader and is severely allergic to neckties!

Bob is so passionate about helping clients build successful businesses and lifestyles by defining and creating their version of success, that he even trademarked his personal philosophy statement... ***Do business on your own terms!***

Get started defining and creating success in life and business on your own terms!

Go to www.BobHoldsworth.com/PEAK and sign up for a FREE 21 minute phone consultation to get you jump started.

You can also download a FREE special edition *Success Factors Wealth Building System*^{sm} **e-workbook.**

IS "DEATH" YOUR BUSINESS EXIT STRATEGY? BUILD EQUITY AND LEAVE RICH!

DAVID H. KLAUS
SBO7˚ SUCCESSFUL BUSINESS OWNER 7 STEPS˚ METHOD

"Start with the end in mind."

— STEPHEN COVEY, *quoting many successful business owners including IBM's Tom Watson, Andrew Carnegie, etc.*

"I LOVE MY WORK and I'll keep doing this until the day I die" is a distressingly common statement we hear during our business owner success mentoring. It's wonderful if you L-O-V-E what you're doing, but what happens if that love diminishes or dies? What if you get tired, bored, sick, divorced, or even die?

Think this won't happen to you? Look around. It happens all the time. Will you and your family continue to live the lifestyle you deserve? Plan now, party sooner!

You and your company are NOT the same thing. Your business exists to support your personal goals. Where are you headed? How does your company support your personal goals? Where and when do you get off the train? *Without a plan, any exit will do.*

This is fundamental. Only you can define your goals and what's right for you, but we'll assume here your goal is to create enough wealth to support your lifestyle – not only to survive, but to truly prosper. Newbies, entrepreneurs, small business owners, and family-owned businesses should all be paying careful attention.

I know the owners of a medium-sized company that has traditionally generated significant profits (a sort of "golden goose"). Every penny the company makes pays for their lavish lifestyle. Now their company is near bankruptcy, and what will they have? No income, no company, and most painful for them, a massive reduction in lifestyle.

Here's their plan: spend every penny. Period. Apparently they haven't acknowledged the inevitable second part of their plan, which is to let their instant greed kill the golden goose from inattention and lack of feeding. What's your plan...?

The endgame (or exit strategy) is the point where you depart from your company in one way or another. This is best to consider at the very beginning, because the sooner you plan, the more options (and profits) you'll have at the endgame. Of course, you can plan any time—you just waste less time and energy if you do it now.

This is not a new or secret concept. Even the Bible says you reap what you sow. So the question is, will you and your family have a great life or a struggle after you divest? Your plan affects how you think and operate, because your perspective makes all the difference. It determines how you build your company, the things you do, the opportunities you pursue, and even more importantly, the opportunities you choose to pass by.

Although focused effort is required to build your equity, it's actually pretty easy to get started and ultimately you'll work less and make more. But when you're totally focused on your daily "product," (pizza, toys, consulting, or whatever you sell) you don't have time or energy to grow your equity. *Don't assume equity growth is the inevitable result of your business activities.*

An extremely profitable, well-run, and documented business *can* grow equity, but it's a lot easier to start with this end in mind. Obviously you'll revise and evolve your plan as necessary. Actually, this *is* the point, since successful business owners understand the value comes from the planning process itself. You can do this easily with a little forethought. In a moment I'll even suggest a possible goal to get your thinking kick-started.

TWO WAYS TO WEALTH: INVESTING AND EQUITY

Let's start with a few simple truths. Money is easier to make than to keep. Experience shows us that income is usually spent, but we're talking here about enlightened self-interest. Investing outside your own company is beyond the scope of this chapter, but can be important to getting and staying rich.

But doesn't it make sense to invest the right kind of effort *inside* your company to ensure you receive the highest possible payoff? You're working your butt off anyway, so why not spend a little time now to ensure you're doing those things that lead to the highest payoffs? We're not talking about *additional* work, just *smarter* work.

You'll never stop looking for new opportunities, but your endgame plan gives you a measuring stick for evaluating those opportunities. It helps you attract financing and keeps you focused on profits – not income, and especially not your gross – to quickly maximize your equity. In fact, a simple litmus test to ask yourself frequently is:

"Would I buy my own company if it was for sale?"

GET A PLAN TOGETHER

Whether you're a newbie or well established, the great news is that your exit plan does not have to be perfect. The most important thing is to be thinking about the issue.

Earlier I promised to offer a possible goal to kick-start your thinking and planning. It's a whole lot easier to write *something* down and edit it than to stare at a blank sheet of paper! How about this for starters:

I will sell my company in five years
for a five million dollar profit.

Your goal translates to: "What do I need to do to ensure my company is sellable for five million dollars five years from now?"

Maybe you'd rather merge, or license your intellectual property, or franchise your operation. Maybe you're satisfied with one million profit; maybe fifty million. Whatever. This is *your* endgame.

Here are some common endgame strategies.

- Sell outright. Take the money and run. Face it; you'll never be able to work for somebody else, because people like us are unemployable. In a few cases you might have physical or intellectual property vital to the buyer, but most buyers are looking for a "franchise-quality" or "turn-key" operation.

- Sell your intellectual property.

- Collect royalties or licensing fees on your intellectual property.

- Merge with another business.

- Most difficult, but with the greatest potential return, is to go public. This is a whole different universe and won't be further discussed here.

- Shut down your company and sell remaining assets for their salvage value, if you're lucky. This is the default outcome for those who aren't exceptionally lucky and have made no plan. *Don't let this be you!*

SYSTEMIZATION IS KEY

Systems are key to both your daily operations and to creating business equity.

The more decisions you must personally make, the harder you work, the greater your stress, and ultimately the less valuable your company is. Identify, test, validate, and document every process as if you intended to create a franchise business. Who knows, you might *actually* later decide to franchise your company or intellectual property. Regardless, you'll come out ahead when you operate by systems.

When your company is extremely profitable with minimum input from you, it's easy for somebody else to step in and buy it. Here's a rule of thumb: if, after three years, you're still making all the decisions, *you've built a job and not a business*. Remember, potential buyers are usually looking for a turn-key operation, and if you're still the key player you'll end up working for somebody else.

Your marketing system is probably the most critical system your company must have. Don't forget your administrative systems. How does your office operate? If you have a store or production facility, how does it operate? Identify and document every process. Not only do these become your training manuals for new employees, it's easier to replace an employee when necessary. You're creating ready-made intellectual property you can license or sell.

OTHER CRUCIAL FACTORS

Branding is essential, but be careful. Your personality defines your company, and you will probably be the public face of your company. But be very careful to distinguish between your company and "you" in your branding.

If "you" *are* the company, what's left for the buyer when you leave? Exactly what is he buying? In relatively few cases branding with your "name" can work (Dan Kennedy and Bill Glazer, for example), but not often. The internet marketing world, for example, is filled with marketers who have failed to create company identities separate from themselves. When they leave, what's left?

A positive example is Papa John's Pizza founder John Schnatter. His first name, face, and personality are certainly the public persona of the company, but he has created a company that he can easily sell. Like

KFC's Colonel Sanders, John could be well paid to remain the face of the company without remaining *in* the company. What a great income stream!

Retain ownership and control in your company…unless you're looking for long, sleepless nights of stress, pain, argument, and probably years of litigation. If you don't own the company, how are you going to sell it? If you don't control it, will you be allowed to sell it?

Your customer list and relationships are vital property. They're obviously important in your day-to-day operations, and a prospective buyer is going to be much more interested in a large, active customer list than no list or an old list. It's also crucial to care for and feed your total customer value. This is defined elsewhere, so we won't discuss it here. Maybe size matters, but quality and value are paramount!

If you're getting paid cash at the endgame, get all of it up front —or at least as much as possible. Business buyers are notorious for failing to make their installment payments. Too often the buyer runs your old company into the ground and can't pay the installments. Get your money now and laugh all the way to the bank.

You'll need first-class legal and accounting advice. It's worth your time and money. Create a watertight agreement for ending the game. Your professionals aren't entrepreneurs and won't be able to empathize with you, but you need their technical expertise and advice — even if you choose not to follow it.

Make sure that they are capable, qualified, and experienced in the precise areas where you need their help. You have to live with the consequences, not them. You need their best work, and should be willing to pay for it.

David H. Klaus is a successful business owner, mentor, consultant, and creator of the SBO7™ Successful Business Owner 7 Steps™ Method, at www.Successful-Owner.com. He is also the creator of the SBO7 RFM Method™, an extremely easy-to-use process for business owners to identify and connect with their best customers, lost customers, etc.

NOW FOR THE FREEBIES!

To truly kick-start your endgame thinking, visit www.Successful-Owner.com/SPPgiveaway/ to claim your FREE copies of my "7 Deadly Endgame Mistakes" report, user-friendly worksheets for your stage of business (exploration, startup, growing, mature), and a bunch more useful stuff!

SOCIAL MARKETING TRAFFIC MACHINE

MARITZA PARRA & JEFF HERRING

Traffic.

We use strange words on the internet, don't we?

Traffic is usually something we want to avoid. Yet on the internet it is the lifeblood of your business. There are some that would sell their soul for more traffic.

The good news is that you do not have to sell your soul for more traffic. There are so many powerful and free ways to get all the traffic you could ever want or need.

The first thing I learned about traffic when I started working online was this quote:

> *"Don't chase after traffic. Find out where the traffic is going and get in front of it"*

One of the easiest ways to do this is with Article Marketing and Social Marketing.

30 MILLION UNIQUE VISITORS A MONTH

Article Marketing is the best way to get free highly qualified traffic. EzineArticles.com is the number one Article Directory on the Internet, currently receiving, at the time of this writing, 30 million unique visitors a month. That's a million a day. Or 41,666 an hour. Or 500 in the time it takes you to read this article.

This is the epitome of "finding where the traffic is going and getting in front of it!"

And all you really have to do is write conversationally, or write like you talk. The quickest and easiest way to craft a bunch of good quality articles is to use 3 of my most powerful Article Creation Templates.

1. *7 Tips* – Come with 7 tips about a specific topic in your niche. Then craft 60 or more words for each tip and then you are done.

2. *3 Stages* – Identify a problem or challenge in your niche. Break the problem down into 3 stages such as mild, moderate and severe. Identify the signs and symptoms of each stage and what to do instead.

3. *3 Mistakes* – Come up with 3 of the most common mistakes people make in your area of expertise. It's difficult to resist a title such as "Which of These 3 Deadly Mistakes are You Making In (fill in the blank)." Describe the mistake and be sure to include what to do instead.

This appears as if it gives you 3 good quality articles. Actually it can give you 16. The 3 original articles, then an article on each of the 7 tips, an article on each of the 3 stages, and an article on each of 3 mistakes.

"AND NOW I'D LIKE TO INVITE YOU TO..."

At the end of every article you are allowed to have up to 2 active links back to your website, blog, or other Social Media channel.

This part of the article is called the Resource Box. It needs to flow naturally out of the article and into your links.

You can model this on one of my Resource Boxes that is responsible for roughly half of my list community:

"And now I would like to invite you to claim your Free Instant Access to two of my Instant Article Creation Templates when you visit http:// TheArticleGuyBonus.com

You'll get two "plug-n-play" article templates - just plug in your info! And you will also get a 30 minute Audio Replay of a teleseminar about writing more articles in less time than you ever thought possible.

From Jeff Herring - The Article Marketing Guy and The Great Article Marketing Network."

SOCIAL MARKETING SIGN POSTS

Now because of the amount of traffic you get from EzineArticles, your article by itself is a great source of traffic.

And it's about to get better.

Because the next question is "How do I get even more traffic to my articles?"

ENTER SOCIAL MARKETING

Some folks still think that Social Marketing is just a passing fad. I have three things to say about those folks:

1. They are wrong.

2. They are your competition.

3. This is a good thing.

Think of every Social Marketing platform as a sign post directing traffic to your articles and more.

Here are just four Social Marketing tools that you can leverage as sign posts directing traffic to your articles. Included is their Alexa.com ranking – Alexa.com ranks the amount of traffic a website receives. The lower the number the more traffic, so Number one is best and that is currently held by Google.

Facebook (#2) - Create a Fan Page on Facebook. Announce to your fans when you are working on a new article. This builds anticipation for your article. Then when your article is done and published on your blog or EzineArticles, post the title of your article with a link back to your article.

You could also have a regular feature on your Fan Page where on a certain day of the week you published a new article link. Your readers come to anticipate your next article and are eager to return and read it.

If you include the link to your article in EzineArticles.com, it will display as a graphic with the title on your Fan Page. This is nice "eye candy" that attracts the eye of your reader and prospect.

YouTube (#3) - With todays' technology and tools, you can quickly and easily create Video Articles out of your best articles and upload them to YouTube. We were raised on TV and YouTube is just another version of that powerful screen. Use it.

If you are cringing at the idea of putting yourself on video, relax. Even if you believe you have a "face made for radio" you can create Video Articles. Simply take one of the points from your article and create a few Power Point slides around that point. Use a screen capture software tool such as Camtasia to record your screen. Upload the video to YouTube and you are broadcasting all over the world.

And getting the traffic that comes with it!

Be sure to include a link to the original article in the description of your video.

Twitter (#11) - Twitter is a gold mine for redirecting traffic to your articles. Here is what we recommend:

When you sit down to create an article, announce it on Twitter. Say something like "Just starting on a brand new article on _____ - watch for it.

When you submit the article to EzineArticles.com let your Twitter following know about it. You can say "I just submitted a brand new article on _____ - should be out soon.

In this way you are building anticipation for your new article.

The nice thing about having your articles on EzineArticles is once you set up your account correctly they will "auto-tweet" your new articles for you. In other words, they will send an announcement that shows up in your Twitter stream announcing your new article. Here is the link to a video that shows you exactly how to do this: www.JeffHerring.com/autotweet

Once a new article is out, either on your blog or on an Article Directory, announce that the article is available. Then make multiple follow up announcements throughout the next few days as well. Use quotes from your article and include the link. Ask "Have you seen this yet?" and direct them to your article.

The thing to remember about Twitter is that it is very fluid. So an announcement you make one day in the morning might not be seen by someone who will see a similar announcement that you make the next afternoon.

LinkedIn (#27) – LinkedIn.com is a great source of business traffic and is ranked in the top 30 websites in the world in terms of traffic. They have combined some of the best features of Facebook and Twitter to increase the power of their platform.

You can announce new articles on LinkedIn and direct your connections to your article through a link. You can also set up your LinkedIn account so that each of your new tweets on Twitter show up on LinkedIn too. This can be great because now you can have a new article come out on EzineArticles, and announcements about the article show up on Twitter and then LinkedIn automatically.

This just serves to drive more traffic to you and your articles.

Leveraging Social Marketing tools allows you to not only get in front of where the traffic is going, you can then direct that traffic exactly where you want it to go.

If you used just one of these strategies you would get more traffic. I wonder what would happen if you used all of them?

And now we'd like to invite you to claim your Free Instant Access to the 3 Part Social Marketing Blueprint Video Training series when you visit http://SocialMarketingBlueprint.com/peakbook

You'll see how to leverage Social Marketing tools for traffic and profits.

From Maritza Parra & Jeff Herring and the Social Marketing Blueprint.

Maritza leveraged one little known Social Marketing tools *to get Oprah to call her* for an interview. Maritza teaches social marketing, video creation, and how to turn your expertise into profitable information products and services.

Jeff's students and clients discover how to create more content in less time, build a strong online presence, generate a massive flow of traffic, build a highly qualified and highly responsive list, and create multiple information products to build their information empire.

Together Maritza and Jeff have created the Social Marketing Blueprint and the Social Marketing Platinum MasterMind. One of their favorite activities is holding exclusive workshop retreats at Maritza's Hacienda in San Antonio, Texas, where participants create their online business in a weekend. They live in Atlanta, Georgia and San Antonio, Texas with two boys and three dogs, one of which has his own blog.

HOW TO USE POSTCARD MARKETING TO INEXPENSIVELY & EFFECTIVELY BOOST YOUR MARKETING RESULTS

GRANT MILLER

DON'T BE AN ADVERTISING VICTIM!

For more years than I wish to think about, I was an advertising victim. A victim of listening to what the ad salesperson said to do or even worse, let them write the ad themselves. No offense to them but they were hired to SELL ads and I'm pretty certain they couldn't write an effective ad if their life depended on it.

Radio, TV, newspaper, yellow pages, Val Pak, you name it… I wasted literally hundreds of thousands of precious advertising dollars on poor performing, ineffective, and un-trackable forms of advertising.

Eventually after years of studying the tried and true methods of the old masters and their contemporary counterparts, I now ONLY spend my own marketing dollars if and only if every dollar is accountable and measurable.

Using the proper marketing techniques can make any ad effective and will work in most forms of media. That being said, I especially like using these techniques for postcard mailings. Postcards are an excellent choice for many reasons:

- Relatively inexpensive to produce (as low as 6 or 7¢ each in quantity)

- Very fast to produce

- Able to use pictures, graphics, bold headlines & offers that get your customers' attention

- Lower mailing cost than a letter

Postcards come in many sizes and varieties: 4 x 6, 5 x 7, 5 x 9, 6 x 11 and more. One color, two color, full color, gloss or flat finish, the options are numerous to suit your needs.

WHAT SHOULD THE POSTCARD SAY?

Personally, I like to use a little humor and/or be a little outrageous with my mailings. I really think that most people take things way too seriously and for my main business and demographic of customers, humor is acceptable and appreciated. In your business, the humor approach may not be quite as appropriate but you certainly can still use a postcard very effectively.

I also strongly recommend using some of your own personality in your marketing. People like to deal with people, especially people they know and feel good about. You can actually make yourself somewhat of a local celebrity which will also increase the effectiveness of your marketing overall. Using pictures of yourself, your dog or cat can easily be incorporated into the postcard and make it much more personal and interesting.

Once you are a customer of mine you'll receive no less than 14 postcard mailings a year. I typically send some sort of offer once a month based on a holiday sale, promotion or event.

I'll also send a special Thank You postcard which offers a Loyalty Reward Discount to customers who made a purchase in excess of "X" amount the previous month. Very typically, someone who just spent money with you is likely to spend even more with you. This particular postcard encourages and actually rewards them for doing so. It's highly effective and the customers really appreciate it.

MY SECRET WEAPON

One of my "secret weapons" has been the Birthday Postcards. We collect birthday information on every new customer. If you aren't collecting birthday information from your customers, you need to start immediately. The birthday postcard mailing gives them a totally FREE offer. This is kind of reminiscent of when I was little kid and Baskin Robbins gave you a free kiddie cone on your birthday. People love to be remembered on their birthday and everyone loves something for free with no strings attached.

The birthday postcards I send automatically bring in at least a $8 to $1 return on investment every single month. So for example, every $100 I spend sending out these postcards brings in at least $800 in measurable and trackable revenue. If you do just one kind of mailing, I strongly urge you to do a birthday offer. And don't be cheap, give them something totally free and of real value. Besides the great ROI we receive, we also receive tons of good will from the customer, which is created for free.

Since the birthday mailing is so effective, I also send out a ½ birthday postcard offer six months before their next birthday. When we were little, we would always want to be older. So instead of being just six years old, we were six and a half. This postcard mailing gives the customer a special "half off" offer to celebrate their half birthday! It's almost as effective as the birthday postcard and once again, the customers get a real kick out of it.

I also send postcard offers on their anniversary of first doing business with us and when we haven't seen them for a while.

To reactivate long lost customers, I created a sequence of four different postcards that are mailed out in specific time intervals. Each postcard has a "sorry you're lost," "we miss you" or "we're looking for you" theme to it. Here's a very interesting thing to take notice of regarding a sequence of mailings. Typically three or four mailings to a person will double or triple response rates. Most business people think that you just mail to them once and if they don't respond, the customer is just not interested. This simply is not the case. Multiple mailings (done properly) will always increase your response results.

HOW TO CREATE AN EFFECTIVE POSTCARD

There are multiple factors that will have an immense impact on your results. Listed below are some of the most basic characteristics that your postcard must include in order to be effective:

- The Headline – This is the most critical element. The job of the headline is to get the person to read the rest of the postcard.

- The Story – This is your reason for sending the postcard to the customer. Holidays are a great reason for you to be contacting them and there is always a holiday going on. Sometimes the best holidays are ones that no one ever thinks about like National Compliment Day, National Nurse Anesthetist Week, Betsy Ross' Birthday, Fun at Work Day (all in January by the way).

- The Offer – This is what you are trying to sell and want your customer to buy. Ideally it will be an "irresistible offer," something that they just cannot pass up. Since you never know which side of the postcard your customer will see first, I strongly recommend putting the offer on BOTH sides.

- The Deadline – Without a deadline nothing usually ever gets done. We all tend to put stuff off until we have to. The offer doesn't mean very much unless you include some sort of deadline. The deadline can take many forms….time, limited quantity, reward for fast response, etc.

- Guarantee – Most anything that you sell or do can be guaranteed in some way. You will sell more if you can guarantee it.

- Photos/Illustrations – One of the best reasons to use postcards is the ability to use a picture or illustration to get your message noticed. The photos can take up the entire portion of the postcard or just a small part of it. Either way, it will dramatically increase the effectiveness of the message/offer.

- Cosmetics – Using cosmetics effectively will increase the readership of the card and allow you to highlight key points. Some examples of cosmetics would be sub-heads, bold-facing, bullets, underlining, handwritten fonts, font sizes, colors, etc.

- The Close - You need to tell them exactly what to do next. Stop in, call this number, go to a website, bring this postcard with you in order to redeem, etc.

- Other Elements – Space permitting, depending on the size and format of the postcard you are sending, you could also include one or more PS's, testimonials, credibility builders and personalization.

As with most forms of media you will get the best response mailing to existing or previous customers. Mass mailing an entire geographic area or zip code(s) of non-customers will most likely not be profitable. There are other methods such as two step lead generation ads in a magazine or newspaper that is much more cost effective.

I send out letters during the year also. New members get a "Welcome Letter," we send membership re-activation letters, a monthly newsletter and others. Although you never want to rely on any one type of media exclusively, postcards offer a fast, inexpensive, and most importantly, an effective method to sell to your customers, clients, members or patients.

FINAL WORDS OF WISDOM

ANY type of business can easily benefit from a structured postcard mailing system. It's easy and effective once you know how to do it properly. Now you know a Peak Performer secret to make sure that you will not become an advertising victim. Implement this strategy as soon as possible and you will also begin to maximize your business' profits.

Grant Miller is a serial entrepreneur living in Erie, PA. Grant's early business experience came primarily from growing up in his parents' various businesses. At the age of 25 he started a video store business which grew to be the largest chain of video stores in Northwestern PA. Reel Entertainment Video was ranked in the top 100 video store chains in the country.

As the video store industry began to change, Grant experimented by placing four stand-up tanning booths into one of his video stores. Within a couple of years, using Glazer-Kennedy style marketing, he built the largest and most luxurious tanning salon chain in the area. Sun Your Buns is consistently ranked in the Top 250 Tanning Salons in the country and #1 in Erie, PA.

Using postcards to effectively acquire new customers and to get current customers to spend more and more often is just one of the tools in his fast & easy marketing system. Grant now consults and teaches other tanning salons, hair & beauty salons, spa owners, retail and service businesses how to grow and maximize their business profits using proven Glazer-Kennedy style marketing.

For more FREE resources on how to market your salon, spa, retail or service business go to:

www.TanningSalonMarketing.com

THE ULTIMATE EXIT INTERVIEW: THE WAY TO PREPARE YOU AND YOUR FAMILY

TIM PELTON

UP FRONT AND TO THE POINT, my goal is to challenge you to plan for the needs of your family when you die.

Without being melodramatic, what if you suddenly died of a heart attack today or were struck and killed by a drunk driver on the way home? Could your family manage all your affairs once you are gone? Eight out of ten people I have spoken to state that they have never thought about it, let alone planned for it.

It is ironic that we all spend countless hours supporting our kids, including fulfilling transportation needs that would challenge NASA, standing in the rain through numerous athletic competitions, and running the gauntlet of the college application process. We plan vacations with intricate details to maximize the needs of each member of our family.

And yet none of those events are preordained. The reality is that we are all going to die. *The reality check is that most people have done no planning for this **guaranteed** event.* Culturally, death has always been a taboo subject to discuss and it is considered too macabre to talk about it.

It's time to get over this behavior.

Let's begin by exploring an easy question.

DO YOU NEED A WILL?

Absolutely. Otherwise, once you pass away you have no control over the distribution of your assets.

Important Note: I am not an attorney, nor am I providing you with a legal opinion. What I am giving you is practical advice from the 'school of hard knocks.'

If you die without a will, the term is called *Died Intestate*. Your estate is divided according to Intestate Law. Your family does not have a say in directing who gets what, your state will. The spouse *may* get some assets if they are held jointly. If it is an asset held separately, then some portion *may* go to your spouse and some portion *may be* distributed amongst the kids or folks you desire assets to go to. But fear not, the government will step in to manage the situation and we all know "the government is here to help."

My simple advice is to work with your attorney to craft a will that meets your goals. If your estate and asset holdings are not very involved, you can check out www.legalzoom.com and www.legaldocs.com for online wills that you can download.

A will is a very important document to prepare. It's a no brainer…**do it**.

Now let's move on to a much more difficult question.

WHAT FUNERAL ARRANGEMENTS WOULD YOU LIKE WHEN YOU DIE?

When I ask people if they have a will, clearly most folks get a little uncomfortable. When I inquire if people have thought about planning their funeral, everyone gets squeamish. But take a moment and think of it from the perspective of your surviving family members who desperately want to do the right thing for you when you pass away. Do *they* know what your funeral wishes are?

- Do you want to have a wake?

- Do you want to have a funeral service?

- Do you want to be buried in a casket or cremated?

- Do you want to use the local cemetery?

- Do you want your funeral to be elaborate or low key?

As challenging as these questions may be, think of the burden it adds to your family, during an incredibly stressful period, if they are unaware of your funeral desires.

WHY AM I SO PASSIONATE ON THE SUBJECT OF PLANNING FOR THE DAY YOU DIE?

Actually there are several reasons. First and foremost, I am the sole survivor of a family of five. Both my parents, an older brother, and an older sister have all died due to health related complications. With all of today's modern life-extending technology, I still appreciate that acknowledgement of your family's medical history plays a big part in one's own health…and future!

Also, with over 20 years in the fire service, I have witnessed way too many people who died needlessly or due to irresponsible behavior. The surviving family members always have the same two questions: (1) Why!? and (2) What am I supposed to do next?

I had a near death experience when I seriously thought all my chips might be cashed in. Sunday, March 31, 1991 dawned sunny, clear, and warm. It was going to be a great spring day. It was Easter Sunday. A fire alarm came in for a car fire which is really a fairly routine call. However, in the panic of the moment, the homeowner had failed to inform the 911 dispatcher of a significant detail. The car fire was inside the attached garage of a four-bedroom home.

I was a Captain at the time, and was given the search and rescue assignment to search the second floor for two boys that were unaccounted for. The homeowners could not confirm if anyone was upstairs.

Heavy black smoke had banked down to the floor at the top of the stairs and we had to don our breathing gear right away. About 7-8 minutes into the search, my partner's breathing apparatus had a major failure and he was getting very little air. He had to get out and get out fast.

There are two *absolute* rules in the fire service:

> Rule #1: **Never** leave your partner
>
> Rule #2: **Never** violate Rule #1

THE ULTIMATE EXIT INTERVIEW: THE WAY TO PREPARE YOU AND YOUR FAMILY

However, when you are a new Captain, on an adrenaline rush, thinking you are immortal, have not completed your mission—you sometimes make foolish decisions. I elected to continue the search – *alone*.

Visibility was zero and suddenly I was disoriented. I felt like I was trapped in a phone booth. My knees and back were burning and every direction I turned seemed to be a dead end. Worse…I suspected that no one knew exactly where I was. I began to panic. Then my low-air alarm on my breathing apparatus went off. I thought of my wife and daughter and thought 'Great, now every Easter from here on out is going to be remembered as the day Dad died in a fire!'

I was scared and could feel stomach bile backing up in my throat.

In an effort to quell my panic, I remembered a trick one of the "old guys" had taught me. If you're about to panic, close your eyes and count to ten. I thought he was nuts at the time, but at this point I would try anything. I did it, and it worked! It gave my brain a time-out that triggered my need to survive and outweighed my panic. If I made all right hand turns going in this room, then making all left hand turns should get me out.

My air supply ran out as I passed through the front door into the yard. I remember throwing up all over a budding rhododendron bush.

By the way, no one was upstairs. The unaccounted for boys were at a friend's house.

It took me a long time to talk about such a horrendous mistake with my colleagues, let alone my family. But if there is a gift I took away from that event it was the fact that I am not immortal and I started to think about what needs to happen after I die.

The thought process has evolved into two publications: *The 11 Things You Absolutely Positively Must Do Before You Die* and (coming soon) the comprehensive *Ultimate Exit Interview Workbook* and CD set. The workbook covers everything from detailed funeral arrangements to creating a comprehensive financial plan. Think of it as the ultimate exit strategy.

Lastly, my most passionate interest in planning for the day you die has been driven by my direct involvement following the attack on America on 9-11. Within 24 hours of the attack and based upon some specialized training, I was on-scene at Ground Zero providing mental health support to emergency service personnel.

We each have our own images of that horrific day. And yet my most vivid images have little to do with the carnage and destruction. I will always 'see' the desperate struggle of family members and co-workers, in the days following the attack, desperately seeking to know the whereabouts of a loved one.

In New York, 2605 civilians, 60 police officers, and 343 firefighters perished. Additionally 125 people died at the Pentagon and 246 souls died aboard aircraft. Each person was simply going to work and never came home. Most never had the opportunity to say 'goodbye' or 'I love you.'

ASKING THE HARD QUESTIONS

I can vividly remember when I first broached the question of funeral planning with my beautiful bride. I anguished at length at how to tee up the first question to break the ice. With a knot in my stomach and a crack in my voice I asked "Have you ever given any thought about what you would like to have happen when you die?" Her answer was immediate and almost blasé. She said "Sure, I want to be cremated." (*Wow, that was easy,* I thought to myself.) Pressing on, I inquired where she would like her remains to go. In the same sentence she said "Well let's see. We've lived in the same town for over 30 years; let's buy a plot in a cemetery here. I'm going shopping…bye."

Getting started may be easier than you think.

Fortunately you now have a choice. You have an opportunity to lighten the load your family and friends will carry when you pass away. It's not about you…it's all about them.

Have the courage to do the right thing.

NEXT STEP

Have the courage to ask yourself this simple but hard question: *What do I want to happen when I die?* Then have the compassion to share your answers with your family. The benefits you will reap are beyond description.

Unfortunately, space limitations in this chapter preclude me from sharing some additional aspects of *The Ultimate Exit Interview*. Examples of some additional topics include financial planning, estate planning, and business succession planning.

NEED HELP GETTING STARTED?

More detailed information is available in my book, *The 11 Things You Absolutely Positively Must Do Before You Die.* The book is available *at no cost* at my website www.timpelton.com/11things.

In closing, have the courage to begin to ask yourself, "What do I need to do to protect my family when I am not here?" I acknowledge that some of the questions may be hard. But not addressing them will be harder.

"There are no easy answers but there are simple answers. We must have the courage to do what we know is morally right."

— RONALD REAGAN

Respectfully,

TIM PELTON

Founder, Ultimate Outcomes, LLC

Tim Pelton is a veteran entrepreneur, business owner, devoted dad, lover of life, former fire chief, and great leader that knows how to have fun along the way. He believes his mission on this earth, and therefore his passion, is helping people.

He has been fortunate to have had a very diversified career in management and leadership in both the public and private sector.

As a business owner and entrepreneur, his expertise has involved strategic planning, resource allocation, and a sophisticated high-end, customer service oriented style. His unique management philosophy is very simple: lead from the front, pick good people, and have fun.

Life is too short not to have a good time.

HOW TO EAT AN ELEPHANT

DR. GLENN SCHMIDT

YES, HOW DO YOU EAT AN ELEPHANT? As you read this article, you will realize why it is important to know how to eat an elephant and why the answer is **important** for you and your business.

If you are reading this, you are likely to be a businessman, businesswoman or an entrepreneur looking for an advantage or an idea to make your business better and more productive. You want to succeed and you have the ideas and the drive to make your business more successful or to expand or start your business. You want to make your first million. Most people want to make it big but, unfortunately, most fail and sometimes fail miserably. What happens to cause the failure or to produce meager results? Why do some guys become extremely successful while others fail? If you ever ridden on a steam locomotive, the difference between the train moving and not moving is a matter of only one degree Celsius. That's right, just one degree. Water will boil and create steam to move the train at 100 degrees Celsius. If the temperature is 99 degrees or less, there is no boiling water and no train moving. One degree makes the difference. Your business is similar to that train. You can put in the effort, but if you don't have that one degree difference, you won't make it. What is the one degree difference? There are many components, but today I am going to give you one of the most important.

Surprisingly, the answer to the one degree difference is everywhere. How many football games are decided by the runner making that one yard to make the first down and giving the team impetus to score? How many basketballs just barely drop in and decide a game? Your business is composed of parts, often times small and maybe not even related, but, just like a football team that is efficient and plays a great game or the basketball team that can score and play defense, your team has to have all its parts working together. Too often, you, as a business owner or entrepreneur, look at the big picture and don't see the small parts that need extra attention or effort to give you the extra STEAM to make your business run.

In my profession, the standard of success is to have a million dollar a year practice (I am a dentist). However, most dentists don't really understand what it takes to make a million dollars a year, and most don't make a million dollars a year. In your business, do you know what it takes to make $100,000, $500,000, $1,000,000 or more a year? There is a simple answer to this question. Most people would look at the million or $100,000 as a whole number, a mountain to climb, an obstacle to overcome. Most people won't or can't climb the mountain or overcome the adversities in their way. I ask you now, what is the easiest way, as a businessman, to make your first million or get a record number of sales or subscribers? Most of you do not know the answer.

If you look at a million dollars as a whole, it can look like a lot of money, especially if you are selling $29.95 widgets. However, I am going to tell you that the easiest way to look at your goal of a million a year is to look at what it takes to make it. I am not talking about overall effort. What I am referring to is the actual daily effort to make the daily smaller amounts that add up to a million a year. Most people would look at a million and think it is a big number. What I am going to tell you is you need to look at it from a different perspective. For example, if you work five days a week in your business and you want to earn a million dollars a year, all you need to make is only $4,000.00 a day. That's right. If you work 50 weeks a year, with 2 week of vacation, and if you average a five day work week, that is 250 working days each year. Your daily goal of $4000.00 a day will earn you a million dollars for the year. Now, depending on what kind of business you have, making $4000.00 may be a reasonable figure. If $100,000 is your goal for the first year, then the daily goal is only $400.00 a day. What you need to see is that the total goal is not that for which you are shooting. You are shooting for a **daily** goal, keeping it in mind and doing the math, so that your yearly goal is broken down into a doable daily goal. Better yet, if you have an online business that runs 24/7, 365 days a year, and your goal is one million, divide by 365 days and a daily amount of only $2,739.73 is what it will take to make that million.

Obviously many of you are at different levels of business and income. But, if you look at where you are and where you want to be, plan on your business accomplishing that yearly goal by having a daily goal. It's that simple, and the best part of all is this is that it's much easier to make a smaller amount than thinking of that large figure you desire. Too often, large amounts can make things seem overwhelming and unreachable. The secret to really making those large goals attainable is to break it down into its smallest component and strive to make that smaller component **every workday**.

You need to sit down right after reading this article and figure out what your goal is, and it doesn't have to be money. Then, break it down into its smallest part. If you want to have 1200 sales a year, then you need to think in terms of what that is per month and then break it further down into what it really means on a daily basis. For example, if last year your business made 900 sales (which is 3.6 sales a work day) and this year you want 1200 sales, then you and your company have to make 4.8 sales a day to make your yearly goal of 1200 sales, an increase of 1.2 more sales a day.

By taking the big picture and breaking it down into daily components, you can attain your big picture (goal) a lot easier and faster. One thing, however, that you have to do for this to work is to **record** and **monitor** your goal(s) daily, weekly, and monthly. You have to have the info readily available, because you have to look at it every day and see if you made your goal or not. This part is really, really, really important, and noticed I emphasized *really*. You have to keep a running total of your goal and, at any point in time (whether it be weekly or monthly or year to date), you have to know where you are and how far above, even, or below your goal you are. If you don't keep a running total and know these figures, how will you know that you need to make more effort (whether it be more sales call, more mailers, more emails, etc.) or not? I realize some of you are probably thinking of putting it on your computer or excel spreadsheet. I have all that, but I personally prefer a binder that has daily, weekly, monthly, and year to date figures all readily available to be seen at a glance. In fact, to really make this work and to plan your year, as you accumulate information, you should not only keep the current year's data readily available, but also have the data from the previous year(s) next to your present year so you can see if your goal is ahead of the previous year or behind.

It is a fact that people who keep written goals tend to make these goals. Having your daily goal (what that is depends on what you hope to achieve) written down and looked at daily does make a difference. You can obviously have as many written goals as you want. To make it work, however, the goals should all add up to the big picture, i.e. what it is you are trying to accomplish. For my practice, I can tell you what we produced and collected for any particular day, and I can, at a glance, look at and compare a figure to the same time frame a year ago or several years before. That way, I can see any trends for any month of the year. When I plan my next year, I know what the best time of the year will probably be and what I need to do to make any weak parts of the year more productive.

By keeping these kinds of records and monitoring your daily goals, you will achieve your bigger goal. So, to answer the question how do you eat an elephant, I say: one bite at a time.

Dr. Glenn Schmidt is a full time practicing dentist in New Orleans. You can visit one of his web sites by going to www.NewOrleansDentalReports. com. Free reports on different aspects of dentistry are available there. If you want a copy of how he does his daily, weekly, monthly, and year to date monitor, please email him at GVSDOC@aol.com. If you mention you read about this technique in Peak Performance book, and he will gladly email you a copy and show you the format to use. In addition, Dr. Schmidt does business to business consulting to improve sales and performance for both dentists and businesses. If you are interested in finding out more, please contact Dr. Schmidt at his email.

FOR MAXIMUM SUCCESS, COME AS YOU ARE

(OR: HOW TO EXCEL WHEN YOU'LL NEVER, EVER MEASURE UP TO THE NEXT GUY!)

REBECCA SOULETTE

QUICK! TAKE A LOOK AT THE PHOTO on my homepage, www.rebeccasoulette.com (I'm the cute, long-haired brunette with the BIG smile.) What are your assumptions about me? Put together? Energetic? Competent? Go on, JUDGE ME. Intelligent? Driven? Articulate? Outgoing? Successful?

It's not that I don't actually look like that, it's just that only looking at that photo, you might be tempted to make up things about me that aren't true. And, if you're like me, just from looking at that photo, you may be tempted to judge yourself against the person you may assume that I am.

Here's the truth:

I'm sitting here at my desk in jeans and a tank top with a messy, scrunchied ponytail and bare feet. My chaotic and messy desk is decorated with pink plastic shelves and some "You Rock!" stickers and heart-shaped post-it notes. I have posters of The Spice Girls and Star Wars behind me along with a Guns-n-Roses graphite drumstick that I caught during a show that my cat loves to play with. Oh yeah, I suck at formal networking, I hate making follow-up phone calls, and while the majority of successful business people I know barely sleep, not only do I need at least 7 hours of sleep per night, but I really do need a nap in the middle of the day, every day, so that I'm not a useless basket case.

Now, I don't know about you, but to me, that doesn't sound like someone I'd immediately peg as a Peak Performer.

And it turned out that THAT was the biggest hurdle I had to overcome—accepting that I was seriously quirky (like many people are!) and although I was missing what I thought were some absolutely necessary qualities to have if I was going to be a successful entrepreneur, I found out that working WITH those quirks (instead of against them) helped me build a business that's working beautifully for me and for all the amazing people that I serve.

A year ago, I compared myself to the authors of Volume I of this book series and thought, "God, I don't think I could ever be like them. There's no way I could measure up." Clearly, they were highly driven, energetic individuals, who could implement business ideas faster than I could blink and for more hours in the day than I could stay awake and still function properly. Listening to many of them list their many accomplishments and future plans, I honestly felt like a slowpoke and an idiot.

The good news for me was (and is) that my business is all about helping people excel in their lives and in their work based on who they are, what they value, where their strengths lie, and in creating environments where everything that they're not good at is either delegated, redesigned, or eliminated until, no matter how quirky they may be, their lives and businesses function like strong, well-oiled machines.

And like any good Life Coach worth their salt, I walk my talk. Which meant that I had no choice but to level with myself that I wasn't born with what I thought the qualities of a super successful entrepreneur should be. But that didn't mean I couldn't make it work anyway.

So I began the process of sussing out where I was doing well in my business and where I really wasn't. It turned out that on the actual 1:1, group coaching, and the home study product production front, I was excellent. This was good news, since this was the product I was selling. The structure of my days, my aversion to telephone follow up, and the idea that "networking" always has to be a formal affair, on the other hand, were exhausting me. And because my business doesn't yet run without me, I had to make some significant changes.

So the very first thing I did was choose work hours. This may seem like a silly thing to do, at first glance, but I'm an introvert and I need to know when I'm NOT working in order to give myself the space to recharge. The clientele I serve can be extraordinarily demanding—many of them are accustomed to getting what they want when they want it, even if it's 2am. And many folks advised me that I should be CONSTANTLY available for them. However, being available 24/7 flies in the face of everything I stand for as a Life Coach—it would be like selling myself into slavery for my clients and that wouldn't help them or me. Since having thorough boundaries and honoring others' boundaries is actually a good thing that can make everyone's lives run more smoothly and be more fulfilling.

So, instead of choosing hours based on what I thought my clients might want, I chose hours that worked for me—including hours off in the middle of the day for me to take naps. (Crazy, right? But my goal was to get me in optimum form, and naps do the trick!) And the next thing I did, which was probably one of the most important things I have ever done for my business, was to choose my day off.

Most people expect days off to be on a Saturday or a Sunday. But here's one of the odd things about me; I have never been a fan of weekends. I've always enjoyed my life more when I've worked on the weekends and had days off during the week. So, since I decided to keep the office open on the weekend, I wanted to give myself the best possible day off. So I chose Tuesday—the day of the shortest lines at stores, the least amount of traffic, most services I might need are open, and everyone I know is usually free to get together. So Tuesday became my untouchable, hallowed day. And my one requirement for my day off is that I DON'T do any work (unless it truly feels fun to do and ONLY if it energizes me). These schedule changes based on my personal quirks finally gave me the rest I truly needed in order to have as much energy as I had to have be really productive the rest of the week. I have colleagues, business associates, and clients who think it's incredibly annoying and counterproductive (to them!) that I've walled off Tuesdays— but for me, the protected "me" time has only helped my business grow.

Then, to counteract the energy drain of hating to make follow-up calls, I hired an assistant to do it for me (this saved me HOURS of procrastination time and simultaneously helped my clients get everything they need much faster than if I was doing it myself—giving them a better product and giving me MUCH more energy).

Then, I began networking on Facebook. At first, I tried being "professional" on it, but, the truth is, that just isn't me. I'm the girl with the Spice Girls poster and the Guns-n-Roses drumstick for my cat. I decided just to be myself—no posturing, no pretending I was more put together than I am—and you know what? My business has only improved as a result. I'm more energetic because I'm not trying to be someone I'm not, and people are drawn to me because I'm absolutely real. Quirks and all!

It is my firm belief that the most important secret to being a Peak Performer is to be 100% honest with yourself about who you are and what you're capable of. Sometimes it's helpful to look around and see what other entrepreneurs are doing that makes them successful—but sometimes it's even more important to take a serious look at yourself: No posturing, no glazing or glossing over how you behave or what you need to be your best so that you can work WITH your strengths AND your weaknesses to build a sustainable business that works naturally with you.

Checking in with myself and being completely honest with myself remains the MOST important thing I can do to stay being a Peak Performer—because doing so gives me the priceless opportunity to be laser efficient in fixing and course correcting ONLY those things in my business that actually need to be changed. And those things are different for every entrepreneur.

You might be more productive if you went for a run every day at lunch or if you got an assistant to make those phone calls for you that you always mess up. Or perhaps you would be much more productive if you could spend some uninterrupted quality time with your family—you know, WITHOUT the phone. Only you know what you REALLY need to be your best so you can perform optimally while you're at work. But I guarantee, if you are 100% honest with who you actually are and what you truly need, your efficiency, productivity, energy, inspiration, and joy, like mine, will reach higher levels than, I suspect, they ever have before.

Come as you are. Once you tweak from there, you'll be amazed at the progress you'll make!

Life Coach, Rebecca Soulette (Founder of Life Beyond Celebrity Coaching--helping celebrities, entertainment industry professionals, and others in the spotlight live lives they love BEYOND the fame) began working in the entertainment and media industries in 1993 where she was surrounded by top level executives, entertainers, authors, designers, models and rock stars at ASCAP, the Music Video Association, Sony Music Studios, The Grammy Awards, The Espy Awards, The Daytime Emmy Awards, Simon & Schuster, and Tommy Hilfiger. She became a Life Coach in 2003 and merged her two favorite things - entertainment, and personal development.

Rebecca is a Senior Level Certified Coach with Rhonda Britten's Fearless Living Institute, and a graduate of Coach U, the leading global provider of coach training. She has received additional training at the Schools of Coachville, The Relationship Coaching Institute.

Teachers and mentors who have been instrumental to her development as a happy, fulfilled person as well as a coach have been Marianne Williamson, Wayne Dyer, Ram Dass, Caroline Myss, and many others. Rebecca has been practicing A Course In Miracles since 1994.

Rebecca lives in Manhattan and works primarily over the phone, while her clients live and travel throughout the world.

BONUS #1: To receive your FREE subscription to Rebecca's weekly online newsletter, visit www.RebeccaSoulette.com and enter your name and email in the pink sign up box. Need a Life Coach? BONUS#2: Receive your FREE 20-minute consultation with Rebecca by emailing Rebecca@RebeccaSoulette.com or faxing (212) 918-1587.

CHUNK IT!

JULIE STEINBACHER

YOU DON'T KNOW ME, I REALIZE, BUT I WANT TO TELL YOU HOW TO CHUNK YOUR LIFE SO YOU CAN ACHIEVE PEAK PERFORMANCE.

ARE YOU STRESSED AND OVERWHELMED because you cannot get everything done? Are you neglecting yourself, your friends, and your family? Do you feel that there is just not enough of you to go around? Do you try to be everything to everyone all the time? By doing this, you are not truly giving anything to anyone at any time. Chunk it!! Chunk your time, energy, and presence.

You may feel you are doing your best by working harder and longer to honor the commitments to your business and family. Maybe this is what you have always been taught. Work more hours. Work harder. Unfortunately, with this strategy, you are doomed to fail. Your relationships will struggle and your health will suffer. If you do not focus your time, energy, and presence, you will not achieve the financial success and personal happiness you so deserve. If you really want to achieve Peak Performance, chunk your life.

I know. I was there. I lived my life unchunked. I worked long and hard. I worried about my work while I was at home. At work, I worried about how unfair I was being to my personal obligations. I did not focus on one task at work or at home. I tried to get it done all at once because there was so much to do. At that time, I thought multi-tasking and working more was the answer. This belief system just made matters worse.

After the unexpected death of my brother-in-law, I reflected on my life and decided there had to be a better way. I knew I wanted more than what my hurried life was allowing me to give to my work, my children, my marriage, and myself. I started my own elder law and special needs planning law firm and learned quickly the huge, positive impact of chunking my time, energy, and presence. Today I use the principle of chunking to successfully lead four businesses while still finding the time and energy to be a mom, wife, caregiver, friend, and author. I am diligent about working in chunks of time, expending chunks of energy for what is important in my life, and staying present in whatever priority I am focusing on at the moment.

CHUNK YOUR TIME

"Time isn't a commodity, something you pass around like cake. Time is the substance of life. When anyone asks you to give your time, they're really asking for a chunk of your life."

—ANTOINETTE BOSCO[1]

All too often, we have a "to do list" a mile long and an hour here and there between commitments to work on the list. Maybe we attempt to prioritize the "to do list" and even attempt to estimate the amount of time required to complete the top priorities. Then, we think, "Before I start on my list, I'm going to quickly check my email or phone messages." We willingly hand all control of our time and a chunk of our lives to the person who emailed us or left us a voicemail message. Why?

Maybe we are fifteen minutes into working on our first important task and there is a knock at the door, the phone rings, there is a voice over the intercom, or a box pops up on our computer notifying us of an incoming email message. We allow, even invite, these interruptions to occur. We let a chunk of our time, of our life, be ripped away from us. We not only lose the time it takes to respond to the interruption, but we also lose the twenty minutes it takes to refocus our attention.

This loss of our precious time (and money) occurs when we do not chunk our time. We need to separate our days into blocks of time, and then we need to consider at what block of time we are at our best. If we are at our Peak Performance first thing in the morning, we need to decide what task is most important or takes the most concentration. We need to dedicate that block of time to the activity of most importance and difficulty and establish systems to secure the chunk of time. Our system may be to get lost so we are inaccessible to our staff, families, and friends. We may need to lock our door, unplug our phone, and turn off our email.

We need to dedicate certain chunks of time to checking and responding to email, phone messages, and faxes. Technology is changing the way we need to organize our lives. There was a time when communication came by fax because it was urgent. Today the fact that someone faxed something to you is not an indication that it is not at all urgent.

We need to put a stop to interruptions and multiply our productivity. For starters, we should implement the following time chunking principles:

1. Respond to telephone calls only three times a week via pre-arranged phone appointments.

2. Take the hour after lunch to review the morning's emails, phone messages, and faxes. Deal only with those messages that are urgent and set the others aside.

3. Take the last half hour of the day to look at the afternoon's accumulated messages. Quickly handle the most urgent ones and integrate the others into the next day's agenda or, better yet, delegate them to staff.

Some people reading this will think chunking your time in this way is not possible. On the contrary, it is essential to Peak Performance and profitability. Very few things in life cannot wait an hour. A system can be in place to sort through what can wait and what cannot. If someone calls you, the person answering your phone can be taught to respond appropriately to protect your chunk of time even if the call is from your spouse, child, or very important client.

Time Chunking Principle: Look, today, at your calendar and divide your day into chunks of time. Make sure you align your most productive time with your most important task. Don't let technology unchunk your life.

CHUNK YOUR ENERGY

"We either make ourselves miserable, or we make ourselves strong. The amount of work is the same."

—CARLOS CASTANEDA[2]

We easily recognize we have a limited amount of time. We think if we simply had more time, our problems would be solved. Unfortunately, we do not always recognize that we have a finite amount of energy. True, we can refresh or refill our energy level, but there is a cap. Realizing that the amount of energy we have to expend is limited requires us to make sure our energy is not wasted.

We must stop using our energy on negative thoughts, activities, and people. If we go to work and worry about something we cannot change or have not changed, we waste energy. How often do we accentuate the negative and expend a portion of our finite energy doing so? We must stop this. We must either change it or ignore it, but not dwell on it. Wasted energy is not helpful to any of our priorities.

We must plan to spend our energy on those activities that are important to us. If we go to the office in the morning and expend all of our energy, we will not have enough energy to fulfill our commitments later in the day. For many of us, we go to work and come home exhausted, wanting only to go to bed. How fair or helpful is that to our spouses, children, or our businesses?

Energy Chunking Principle: Decide, today, to not waste your energy on negative thoughts, activities, and people. Chunk your energy so you are able to expend your energy on those commitments that are most important in your life.

CHUNK YOUR PRESENCE

"The most important thing in our lives is what we are doing now."

—ANONYMOUS[3]

111

We organize our time and energy into chunks. We put on the calendar how we are going to spend our time, and we are conscious of our energy; however, we are not true to our system. We do not dedicate ourselves to where we are and what we are doing at that moment. We are not present in our chunk. We must fight against this.

We must be fully present where we are. If we are at home, we must be mentally present at home and focus on our priorities at home. If we are at work, we must focus on our priorities at work. Otherwise, we are wasting both time and energy. If we are not able to do this, we are not being fair to either responsibility—the one that should be our focus or the one that is preoccupying us.

We must be fully present in the task at hand. If someone is asking us a question (of course, during a chunk of time designated for questions) as we sit in front of our computer and an email pops up, we must not take our attention from the conversation to the email. If we move our attention to the email, we will not really hear the details of the question. We may give an answer, but it may not be the best answer. Or we may ask the person to repeat the details. We have just wasted our own time and robbed time from the person whose question we were asked to answer.

Presence Chunking Principle: Resolve, today, to be present in your chunk. If at home, be at home. If at work, be at work.

Before knowing and applying these chunking principles, I felt as though there was not enough of me to go around. Thankfully, I learned to chunk my life. I promise if you do the same, you will find there will be a chunk of you for everyone. You will have the time, energy, and presence to achieve peak performance. You will feel less stress and have more satisfaction in all chunks of your life, all while making more money.

So start today— Chunk It!

(Endnotes)

1 *The Nightly Book of Positive Quotations*. Comp. Steve Deger. Minneapolis, Minnesota: Fairview Press, 2009. Print.

2 Ibid

3 Ibid

Julie Steinbacher knows about working long, hard hours and still needing more time. Growing up in a farming community in North Central Pennsylvania, she was taught that working harder was all that was needed. Fresh out of college, she worked over 70 hours a week juggling two jobs. While going to law school in the evenings, she worked full-time and met the demands of being a wife and mother. When she started her elder and special needs planning law firm, she continued using this work approach with mild success and little overall satisfaction because she could not find the time to get everything done. As she learned to manage her time, energy, and presence (the principles of chunking), she quickly grossed over a 7 figure income while working less hours. She then decided to take what she learned in her own business and share it with other attorneys. She is the President of EDLF Publishing, Inc., which provides the Million Dollar Solution, a marketing system for law firms. Also, she conducts a mastermind group for attorneys who want to focus their businesses on long-term care planning. Plus, she and her law partner authored the *Pennsylvania Trust Guide*, a guide for trustees and their advisors, and the *Pennsylvania Special Needs Planning Guide*, both published by George T. Bisel Company, Inc. She is ready to share her chunking principles with you.

Do you want to feel less stressed and get more done in less time? Learn how to chunk your time, energy, and presence to achieve peak performance in just one month! Visit www. chunkyourlife.com to receive your free gift and get started right now. It's time to Get Chunky with It!

MED SPA MARKETING — THE BASICS (WHAT REALLY WORKS)

DR. JAMES TUREK

MARKETING HAS BEEN CLASSICALLY BROKEN DOWN into two phases namely lead generation or getting people to call or come in, and lead conversion getting them to buy. I'll just stick to med spa lead generation from my perspective as a med spa owner and discuss the one most important lead conversion step all businesses should take seriously. The first "given" is that you know the market, which for us is women 39-64 earning over $35K/yr who comprise 90% of our business. I'll try to give some pertinent examples of what I've done that works and some of the sometimes laughable, but costly, mistakes made along the way

In the fickle world of med spas, one thing's for sure …you can blow a lot of money with standard off-the-shelf marketing—ask me how I know this. One of the major problems is that the owner is usually a professional and has an income that can "stand" a lot of loss of marketing dollars before the marketing, or spa for that matter, goes bust. This is compounded by the fact that most professionals are taught absolutely squat about marketing in school so this lengthens the learning and cash-burning marketing curve. In this chapter I'm going to go through my learning curve and outline what marketing really does work and highlight some mistakes, now called "learning opportunities" that I've made.

WHAT *NOT* TO DO FIRST

My first mistake, or learning opportunity if you're an optimist, was purchasing a jumbo yellow pages (YP) ad. The yellow page rep baffled me with all sorts of statistics on how this was how people looked for their medical spa site; at the time (1998) I was only one of two widely spaced spas in the coastal South Carolina area. We had a custom and habit of asking all new customers where they heard about us and... remarkably, not one said "yellow pages." Most said word of mouth or from a post card, or "I'm a family practice patient" of Dr Turek. Well, over the next few years med spas caught on and we had some competition. The YP rep said—well if you want to maintain your position in the book you need to beef up your ad or the "other guys" will get your business. Despite being stunned that I couldn't (yet) track my YP ad as far as new patients, it seems I didn't want my future patients to *not* see my competitors ad before they *didn't* see mine; so I beefed it up—a huge mistake. So, what I've learned, over ten years, is that the sweet spot is a quarter page ad in the "main" yellow pages book in your area and includes a "free" offer for mentioning the ad. We're in a small area and have three phone books and an additional "mini" book that goes in your car. Again, I only put the quarter page biggie in the main book and just a line ad with number and website in the others. By the way, our free offer is for a Visia skin analysis as seen on *Oprah*, and because of that, is easily mentioned and thus tracked by our staff. Next year we'll further tweak our ad by using the GKIC yellow pages guy to sharpen our marketing saw.

The next big marketing item we bought was radio time. Our marketing rep assured us that this money was well spent to "brand" our business; after all we had a cool name…..DermaVogue. We had great ads, with my wife being the voice talent. All our friends heard the ad; the local plastic surgeons (who had no med spa) told me directly that they were "sick" of hearing our ads and er... my wife's voice. I had patients on the family practice side of the clinic hear the ads; my brother-in-law, the lasik (vision correction) surgeon, thought I must be killing it. But, very few new patients mentioned the radio ad. At $1800 a month, I was bleeding cash and just like hitting my head in the V-8 ad, I should have been smacking myself saying "I could have had a Porsche Carrera" for all the money I wasted. Now the radio does have its place. We've successfully used it to directly promote a seminar or to highlight a new procedure with a direct offer. In my mind the best way to use radio is to "sponsor " the weather (or traffic) on the station. Due to the fierce competition with online marketing, some radio stations will offer to do a "price per lead" type radio deal. This is great if you can pre-qualify the patients to your own criteria, usually a three question sequence. This pricing method can be very good for high priced services, or those with a high lifetime customer value; also, you know exactly where that customer came from. One thing we're going to track next is "sponsoring" the weather and offering a "free report" to clients to measure ad response.

AN INTRO INTO DIRECT MARKETING

What we found next, was located by a matter of chance. A friend bought a franchise for a coupon mailer called Valpak. They design your ad and mail it to the amount of zip codes that you pay for along with various and sundry other unrelated coupons. They were actually my first delve into the direct response marketing and correctly suggested that we place an offer with an expiration date on it to increase response and to help ensure that people would keep our coupon around even if they were only remotely interested. We had finally come across ads where we could track response. And we did get a measured response, but I thought was low, perhaps 1%; however, the return on investment was a clear 2-3 to one. I thought if I can get this kind of response mixed in with the plumber and gutter guys coupon, maybe I'd do a lot better sending out a postcard. I did just that, but as I know now a "one-time" mailing is just that. This one-timer was just a shot in the dark with no sequencing and nothing to stimulate further thinking or action for that matter.

Still DermaVogue med spa was doing just fine, in spite of all the efforts to explode our business we stayed the same. In the meantime we were rated the "Best of the Beach" medical spa multiple years in a row beating out the newer med spas opened by the plastic surgeons and local dermatologists. We knew we were giving great service and treatments. Unfortunately, awards don't pay the bills and we were suddenly faced with a revenue decline. This was in the "boom time," not the recent doldrums and I decided, it was time to get a "consultant" in to help or shut it down; after all the lasers were paid for. The consultant decided that it was time for more and better lasers and to do seminars for education and lead generation. At this time I'd gotten some "amazing free" information from the GKIC guys, but I was already $200K down in new laser technology and $32K in consulting. All the consulting help got us barely up to our previous revenue. The seminars paid off somewhat, but we noticed many of the same people came to the seminar because we usually gave away free treatments sponsored by the vendors. These same people were just waiting (after their free dinner on me) for their "free lottery ticket" of Derma Vogue services worth $1000 or so; but never would pony up for an actual treatment outside of the seminar. With the help of some basic GKIC training, I decided to have a low-priced treatment drawing for those that just showed up; we had a slightly higher-end drawing for those that brought a friend with increased chances (and better seminar seating) the more friends you brought. Of course, whoever brought the most friends got recognition and a 'special' gift. Lastly those that signed up for the seminar special got in the platinum drawing for the really good stuff. The best seminar dates appear to be a week or two before Mother's Day and in October when people try to get the best look before the summer and holiday season respectively.

The next big idea we had was to use email marketing to our client base for monthly offers and to keep them up to date on the latest treatment and health information. We've found the best frequency for this is every two weeks or the "opt-outs" increase. It is imperative to give meaning-ful content on each and every newsletter. Once, without my approval, sent out a frank ad for the monthly specials; this really incensed our regulars who felt like they were betrayed and treated like lowly "cus-tomers." It's important to go through your email statistics after you send a campaign out; you need to track the open rate for the email. We use "Constant Contact" as our email program and this feature is built –in and quite easy to use. We now include one person's initials in the email to receive a valuable coupon for money off their next treatment (or they can bring a friend and double the coupons value).

One of our latest successes was from our hard copy newsletter. We found true the fact (probably from GKIC) that many people...still... weren't on email and preferred a mail-type item. We had a sweet deal with a company that had all the "prettys" a spa newsletter could want.

All I had to do was write the lead article and send in the monthly specials. One downfall was that the newsletter contained only spa and beauty info and no other content to keep people engaged. So, the newsletter probably had a shorter half-life than if it had a broader range on the interest of personalization. The company that produced that newsletter went bust and we, pretty much, were left in the lurch. We initially (and falsely) thought we could get by without a newsletter, but soon realized a 10% decline in business. People actually asked "where is your newsletter." We have just started using a newsletter service by Jim Palmer (thenewsletterguru.com) which we feel will give us the variety we need, that will perhaps get people to pass around our newsletter and receive our company message – and monthly specials.

We spent most of our time on newsletters, e-mails, post cards, seminars and even giving free treatments to our referral sources as part of a referral program. Every month usually has a holiday or something to write about or offer a free bonus for treatment purchased. We are of the mindset that it's better to give a free-mium (free stuff with purchase) than a discount. Giving discounts commoditize's the business and leads to a "Wal-mart" mentality about pricing. Lastly we do use a birthday and half-birthday (thanks Bill Glazer) mailing to get people to come in when they feel they should be treating themselves to something nice. This works surprisingly well.

Hand in hand with email marketing is pay per click (PPC) marketing. About 60% of the people who find us now say they found us on the web. Earlier in Derma Vogue's marketing history, we "tried" PPC advertising and got killed using brief keywords that cost a lot and sucked cash like a government bailout. Now we just try to capitalize on our larger grossing services using long-tail keywords, for example, "fractional CO2 Myrtle Beach" rather than the shorter, generic, and costlier "fractional CO2." We can't really say that we've made money on PPC (and not many can…so this may be a place to hold off marketing dollars). People will search out procedures thoroughly before coming in, often going straight back to the laser procedure of interests manufacturer. So, it's important that you're listed on every website of every laser manufacturer who you purchased a laser from for web credibility. Most people will go directly to the laser manufacturer's source to find a properly trained and qualified operator. Since then we have tried to continuously search engine optimize our website, and are currently doing so through our webmaster, and a web company called Frontdesk SEO which specializes in med spa SEO. Brian Horn has a great SEO/Google optimizing system for sale endorsed by the GKIC group, which is great if you're a "do-it-your-selfer." However, I need a "done for you" type system or I'll get bogged down in the petty details of just getting things done and implemented.

So, to summarize what we've done so far: we have identified our target market, located the places to find them, and tried to get the most impressions to them, as economically as possible. We realize that most people use the web to find services such as ours and that web optimization is important to help people find us easily; also, we need to have a small but noticeable presence in the yellow pages. The hard paper marketing via post card lead generation and follow-up newsletter are important, as well as including these in big holiday times such as Valentine's Day, Mother's Day and the fall holiday season. Many people advocate that there's a holiday every month, week or day; this has to be weighed against your marketing budget, tracking your returns on marketing efforts and the tolerance of your target customer to receiving material from you. We've found true the fact that it's best to concentrate a large block of marketing dollars to those that already use our services and are "fans." Ideally all marketing efforts should be posted on a yearly calendar to ensure proper notice and implementation optimization.

So, in summary, you've got your target market for the med spa; you've got your yellow pages presence (with a free offer) and you've been sending out letters and most importantly, a hard copy newsletter. You send planned monthly promotions to your existing base of customers (who like you) and lead generation (for new customers) with specials around the fall holidays and Mother's Day. Now, you've done all that but nothing changes until the phone rings and you have a system to get people to walk through your door and experience your services. The next most important step is to have a system in place for the person that answers your phone. The phone must be answered, ideally within two rings by a cheerful voice saying, "Welcome to {your company} this is {receptionist's name}, how may I help you?" First the reception person needs to give time for a response. Then their goal is to get the person's name and find out how they heard about your place of business (to track marketing dollars). They should then try to get them in for a free consult (or come in to pick up a free report/information) to get your spa's experience. Ideally if they can get contact information to market to them that would be a plus. (Always let them know you will never share their information). A great system I've found is that of Chris Mullins (mullinsmediagroup.com, who has a turn-key phone training package for you as well as a free video seminar on phone optimization.) Her services are well worth it and she will "mystery shop" your spa to tweak your staff and your scripts. Her book *Monkey Business* gives the basics and is a worthwhile read to get your phone system jump-started. The first secret is to have your phone answering "scripted" to make the message consistent and track expenditures on advertising. What you don't want is to produce all the coordinated marketing correctly and have someone upfront sabotage your business. It can happen ….ask me, I know.

Dr. Jim Turek received his undergraduate degree from the University of Michigan where he studied Biochemistry and Toxicology. He went to the military medical school in Bethesda, Maryland on an Air Force Scholarship and then studied Internal Medicine and ER medicine in Texas. He moved to Myrtle Beach, SC with his wife and three daughters. He was Chief of Emergency services and primary care services and was Board-eligible in ER medicine by experience. As a flight surgeon for the A-10 pilots during Desert Shield/Storm he flew in combat support missions with the 1st Special Operations Wing; upon return he finished his Air Force time as an Aerospace Medicine Consultant. Since 1995 he has had his own general medicine and medical spa practice in Garden City, SC. Dr. Turek is a 2nd degree Black Belt in Karate, plays racquetball competitively, and enjoys Crossfit-style exercise. A professed "flavor junkie," he enjoys gourmet cooking with fresh herbs and wine-food pairing. Dr Turek is a Clemson University Master Gardener and enjoys helping others develop a green thumb. He was rated a Best-of-the-Beach Physician in Myrtle Beach for over seven years and recently (3/2009) voted Best Medical Spa. He has completed his training in age-management medicine through Cenegenics, and credits his own Executive Health Evaluation for positive life-changing findings and insights into his own health. Appointments with Dr. Turek are limited at the current time so reserve early so you too can "Live well... Longer" and look your best.

DrJimTurek@gmail.com

THE PSYCHOLOGY OF TELE-THANKS, TELE-VALUE AND TELE-HELP—

HOW TO USE THREE VITAL TELE-KEYS THAT COULD DOUBLE YOUR SALES

RICH WEBB

LEARN THE SECRETS OF HARVESTING MORE SALES directly from your previous marketing attempts by delivering thanks, value and help via the telephone… and don't forget to get your free customized outbound telephone script at the end of this chapter.

Over the past few years as our business clients have shown a tendency to tighten their belts and monitor their marketing expenditures more closely we have looked hard for ways to help them to close more sales *without having to spend more to acquire more leads.*

After testing many different options we learned that there is one specific process—when it is correctly added at the strongest strategic points in the sales process—that has enabled many clients to as much as double their sales… using only their existing prospect and customer lists.

The secret, which is new to most clients, is an innovative way to sell… without really selling. What exactly is it?

DISCOVER THE KEY TO DOUBLING YOUR SALES FROM YOUR EXISTING LISTS

The key is to add a pleasant, helpful, live voice to your marketing which delivers gratitude and added value, as well as helpful education and assistance in solving real problems. If this voice is also willing to really *'hear your customers'* you will have found a 'super-tool' to significantly increase your sales (often as much as double) from your existing list.

By really listening and talking to prospects and customers that are already in your 'sales process system' in the manner described above, you will be harvesting more leads from your previous and existing marketing campaigns and obtain blazing new revenue streams.

One of the greatest human needs is the need to be heard.

When a customer feels they have truly been heard, sincerely thanked and appreciated; at the same time they have been given additional value, benefits and education which solves their problems, relieves their pain, fills their needs or satisfies their desires—all from a personable live voice which places the customer's needs above their own…

Well, when you are able to deliver that entire package of communication to them they will begin to like you, trust you and become sold on your products and services *without* you having to blatantly sell to them.

Your company has *changed* from *'someone trying to sell something to them'* into *'someone who really cares about them'*. This is a huge and significant transformation that takes place in their mind.

IN DIFFICULT TIMES THE TELEPHONE CATCHES HARD-TO-REACH AUDIENCES AND CREATES INTERACTION AND RESPONSE

The most cost effective way to deliver this powerful live human voice is over the telephone. When you offer Tele-Thanks, Tele-Value and Tele-Help over the phone, prospects and clients are happy to listen to you. Delivering thanks, value, benefits and/or help first, without asking for anything in return—sets the stage for creating a logical next step of purchasing additional products or services from a trusted company who has demonstrated they care more about the customer's needs than their own needs.

This is the most pleasant, low-pressure, relationship strengthening, method of **"selling without selling"** you will ever discover. People love to be sincerely thanked, valued and helped.

And if you target the call to respondents from other media campaigns or toward your past and present customers you do not have to worry too much about issues with the Do-Not-Call list.

Tele-Thanks, Tele-Value and Tele-Help are almost magical methods for *raising lifeless prospects from the dead* and *resurrecting past customers*. They can infuse life into relationships which once burned brightly but have been forgotten, abandoned, neglected or ignored.

YOU GAIN FOUR IMMENSE COMPETITIVE ADVANTAGES WHEN YOU USE THE TELE-THANKS METHOD.

1. You receive *instant* and invaluable *customer feedback* which can be recorded and used to improve effectiveness and profitability. The telephone forces *interaction* and *response*.

2. It positions you as *someone who cares person-to-person*—which stands out because almost no one else is taking the time to do it. Customers will notice you are taking time and making the effort to *build personalized relationships*.

3. It automatically improves your *customer retention* rate.

4. It almost always generates *immediate revenue*.

When you script a personable, care-based, phone call in the correct manner it can not only be used to create a friendly relationship, it can be used to create a "High-Trust Purchasing Relationship."

WHAT DO I MEAN BY A "HIGH-TRUST PURCHASING RELATIONSHIP"?

This is a business relationship where a client does not just make a purchase from you but they will buy as much, and as many, of your products and services as they can, as often as they can. *They will also talk about, and refer you to, as many of their associates as they can.*

LEARN ABOUT THE FIVE HIGH-TRUST PURCHASING CONCLUSIONS AND YOUR CLOSING RATIOS WILL SOAR

A High-Trust Purchasing Relationship materializes when your prospects are led to one or more of the following "Purchasing Conclusions." These conclusions begin to take place as personalized one-to-one contacts are delivered with thanks, value, benefits and help *as though they were directly from you.* The contacts should be specifically designed to educate your prospect or client and make them feel *important* and *special*—leading them to these Five High-Trust Purchasing Conclusions.

1. Your company or product is the *obvious* best choice to solve their problem, satisfy their desire or fill their need.

2. You are the expert in your industry who will educate them how to buy and receive the *greatest value.*

3. You can be *trusted* to help them make the best possible decision for *them*…buying from you will be a pleasant, rewarding experience.

4. They will be allowed to feel *they are in control* of the sales process.

5. They feel they have a *personal connection* or relationship with you and want to *remain involved* with you.

Wouldn't you agree that if a client or prospect feels these five things about you — they will feel they have a *Valuable, High-Trust Relationship* with you — and *they will give you as much of their business as they possibly can for as long as they possibly can?*

Today's consumer decides in an instant whether your message has value to them. Customers want to feel that you know them, as well as knowing what they need and what they want. The "Tele-Thanks" approach lets them 'feel' this right up front and engages them because the message is all about them.

Too many media allow a customer to self-select out of the message you want them to receive. By using a phone call they will at least hear the name of your company and the value proposition you offer from a very pleasant voice who will thank them for their interest and interaction. When done correctly this is a pleasant and unique experience for a consumer even if they are not ready or fully qualified to accept your offer.

In difficult economic times this can be especially effective. You can reach people who will not respond to any other media and once they answer the phone they cannot scan past you or ignore you. The phone necessitates an interaction and if you have engaged them by making the call all about them, you will receive valuable feedback and begin building a relationship that will be much deeper than a one-time purchase.

INTEGRATED MARKETING COMBINATIONS ARE MUCH MORE POWERFUL THAN SINGLE MEDIA BLITZES

When you add Tele-Thanks, Tele-Value or Tele-Help based calls to your existing successful sales process it can bring even more dynamic results. Marketing guru Jay Abraham has written that adding a targeted telephone call to a direct mail campaign will often double and sometimes as much as triple the response rate.

Outrageous marketing expert Bill Glazer has stated that when he added a carefully scripted phone call into his existing sales process for his retail info-marketing package he doubled his sales results.

Leads King and search engine specialist Bob Regnerus has discovered that adding a Tele-Value call to his clients' online marketing campaigns can significantly improve the results and often make the difference between success and failure in an online marketing venture.

In short, the personalized, care-based phone call is a dynamic and immensely powerful marketing phenomenon that can be extremely effective in a variety of marketing and sales scenarios.

How can you put this vastly underutilized marketing tool to work for you? How can you use this valuable *information* to make a profitable *transformation* in your business?

HOW TO MAKE TELE-THANKS, TELE-VALUE AND TELE-HELP WORK FOR YOU AND PAY OFF BIG-TIME

There are three basic ways you can accomplish this. The first and most obvious is to make some calls yourself. This would be the most personal approach. Of course, even if you have the time—making outbound phone calls is likely to be one of the things you most hate to do. However, if you are able to do it, I highly suggest that you try it. Even a few calls per month will greatly help you to keep your fingers and attention right on the pulse and heartbeat of the most important feature of your business—your customers.

The second is to learn how to hire and/or train your staff to make service-oriented, value-added, outbound calls that present your sales message subtly and appropriately. This does require some time and commitment to training, management, tracking and accountability. But I have given you a clear outline of the principles to use if you want to be successful in your efforts.

The third is to hire a qualified call center to effectively handle the outbound and/or inbound calls for you. If you choose to go this route here are a few vital facts you need to know.

Many businesses may have had a bad experience if they ever attempted to use a call center. There are many reasons for this but most of them can be avoided if you learn to ask the right questions and you conduct a proper job interview before you hire a contact center.

Most outsource call centers are not infused with the "Tele-Thanks" approach. But if the center is willing to be flexible with their clients they can usually be taught how to use these methods and make outbound telephone profitable for you.

With a little research and effort you will be able to find and train a call center that will use these principles. Wouldn't it be worth it to as much as double your sales results from your existing and past customer / prospect lists?

Rich Webb, creator and author of the *Winning Edge Marketing System-The Marketing System that Never Fails*, is an internationally recognized consultant, speaker and author who specializes in the rare skill of '**How and When to Add the Telephone Into Your Marketing Mix** to maximize your sales results.

He has helped his clients re-claim over seventy-five million dollars in sales from lost or abandoned prospects in the last three years alone. He is the owner of Tele-Help, an Inbound and Outbound Contact Center as well as the CEO of Winning Edge Marketing.

In 25 years of working closely with clients, he has prepared comprehensive marketing plans, lead-generation campaigns, customer relationship programs and necessary supporting marketing copy and sales collateral for more than 320 clients.

Rich has been a member of the National Speakers Association (NSA) since 1999 and has served for many years on the Board of Directors for the Utah Chapter of NSA. His speaking topics include:

- *How to Explode Your Profits Using the Telephone—Inbound and Outbound*
- *How Building High-Trust Customer Relationships Can Put a Million Dollars in Your Pocket*
- *The 12 Guaranteed Money Making Rules of Marketing*
- *The Seven-Up Relationship Marketing Rule—How it Can Double Your Net Profit*

Free Gift: Your own customized outbound telephone script with no obligation if you call Rich Webb at 1.800.299.9081. Ask for your free script ($500.00 value) and leave your contact details.

Bonus gift: Visit www.tele-help.com and download your free call center check list—*12 Things You Need to Know Before Hiring a Call Center.*

SEMINAR MAGIC

SCOTT WESTERMEIER

THE STORY OF HOW A COUPLE OF DENTISTS GREW THEIR PRACTICE THROUGH THE RECESSION USING PATIENT EDUCATION SEMINARS.

HERE'S A LITTLE STORY you may find useful not only in maintaining your business, but growing it in these tough economic times, or anytime for that matter.

As the recession set in late 2008, and the media fueled the fire with their doom and gloom reporting, our normally successful dental practice began to feel the pinch. Patients were putting off dental care that was not absolutely critical. Not good news for a practice that emphasized lots of elective and high-end procedures. We were feeling the need to come up with a new strategy to attract a stronger stream of new patients, which is the lifeblood of a practice like ours and many other professional service type businesses. We also realized this was no time to save money by cutting our marketing budget, but rather increase it if we could. The challenge was to come up with something different, something fresh, but most importantly, something cost effective. If I learned nothing else from my Peak Performer membership, it was the power of masterminding. So with that in mind, my partner, office / marketing manager and I all sat down to fix our problem with some kind of clever marketing campaign.

We were not strangers to the traditional media (TV, radio, direct mail, email, and the web). Our office manager called our attention to something the local ophthalmologists were having some success with. She went on to explain how they held seminars in their office to teach prospective patients about recent advancements in eye surgery such as Lasik. This, of course was not the first time I was a victim of the old cliché, "but my business is different," and it wouldn't work for dentistry.

Who wants to go to a dental office and hear about the latest dental advancements? As it turns out, a lot of people want to know what we can do for them.

The following is my recollection of how we came to realize the single most effective marketing tactic we ever employed. The interesting thing about our journey is that we had no idea what a goldmine it would turn out to be.

First we had to figure out what would get people to come to our office to hear about what we had to offer. The mastermind revealed that there was a lot of noise in the marketplace about dental implants; the noise led to confusion, and confusion led to an opportunity. We would put on a patient education seminar that would explain and clarify how dental implants are used, what they can do, how they can benefit your life, how much they cost, etc.

The date was chosen for our very first in-house seminar and the panic began to set in. How would we advertise it? Who would speak? Who would make the power point? What about A.V., equipment, chairs, signs, reservations, follow-up, testimonials? Arghh! This little party was going to be a lot more work than we had bargained for, but was it ever worth the trouble!

We put a plan together to advertise the event and took reservations for 25 guests. In the middle of a snowstorm, 27 actually turned out and 15 people scheduled appointments at the conclusion of our first seminar. We were blown away! At the time of this writing, 18 months later, we are still realizing revenue generated from that evening.

There's magic in them there seminars! We had no idea how powerful a move it was to boldly announce that we would educate (not sell), and therefore position ourselves as experts in the field.

So whether a prospective client could attend the meeting or not, the status of our dental practice was elevated on scale proportional to our message reach (TV, radio, print, web). We became an overnight *authority* on dental implants in our marketplace. We even had other dentists refer patients to us because we were now known as the "dental implant gurus" in the marketplace.

The first night we bumbled our way through and I think the non-slick, down-home nature of the presentation worked for us. Folks came in, met us, met our team members, saw the office, and got face time with the 'real' patients who offered their testimonials. We fed them treats, gave away door prizes, and just made sure they had a nice experience for exactly one hour. We don't even know how to sell from stage, but we learned how to create an atmosphere where folks felt comfortable to buy. And *that* is the magic that works - that we had not been able to foresee. The intangible benefits of assembling interested, motivated, qualified prospects together in one room is simply amazing.

Consider also the time leveraging. We were able to present to 27 people at one time! The energy of the room and the social proof influenced everyone in such a positive way.

Well we may have been slow to come up with the concept, but we wasted no time figuring out that this should be a regular event and a core strategy in our marketing plan from this point forward. Since that first seminar, we have hosted a similar event every month including December! Our measurable results have been nothing short of amazing with well over a quarter of a million dollars in dental work *netted* out of these little "open house" events in the first 12 months. We are on track to significantly surpass that figure this year as our event management skills develop and mature.

It's important to note that these seminars were not about regular dentistry, they were designed to present and celebrate our specialty services (read "*high end*"). You see, we know our numbers, we know the lifetime value of a client, we know our average case size and we know the average cost to acquire a client. We also know that when we have a room full of the right folks, we can engineer a great experience for them with no pressure to buy—translating into a very profitable hour for us. In fact, we know of no better return on investment than these monthly seminars. We will never stop doing them!

Our success has not gone unnoticed. The copy cats are just appearing on the horizon, but being first to market has its advantages. Our practice consultants (we always have a coach) have asked us to put together a "how to" manual for their other clients so they can experience the success we have. That was a nice compliment, but we really didn't get excited about it until another market approached us – our dental implant vendor. They said they would recommend a "how to" product to their (massive) customer base of other implant dentists. Now we realized that we were on to something! It seemed to us that another dentist could save a lot of time, money, and aggravation if they had a blueprint or a paint-by-numbers easy formula to host one of these magic events themselves. They could certainly benefit from our experience in the areas of planning, marketing, presenting, event managing, and following up – all areas where we have screwed up and subsequently "fixed."

So whether you are a dentist, lawyer, printer, podiatrist, or plumber, you can reap the benefits of hosting an educational seminar where you give valuable information away for free, and enjoy all of the following:

- Positioning as authority and/or expert.

- Publicity for community service.

- Ability to leverage time.

- Presenting most profitable product/service.

- Enjoying referrals of your live guests.

- Presenting/selling to a warm, captive, motivated audience.

- Having fun doing it.

- Laughing all the way to the bank.

The ULTIMATE Implant Seminar Blueprint is a game changer! You may never have an opportunity like this presented to you again. Our comprehensive, slam-dunk system was created, constantly refined, perfected and guaranteed to generate results – if you just follow our success blueprint! The result is a method, a system, a formula that when applied, will generate success over and over again!

This is the biggest no-brainer decision you'll probably ever have to make.

So you have to ask yourself one question – what am I waiting for? … Just do it!

For more information on how to implement this seminar blueprint for your business – go to JustDoItDental.com.

Scott Westermeier DDS is a third generation dentist practicing in his home town community of East Aurora, New York for over 25 years. Recognized as a leading cosmetic and restorative dentist by both community and peers, he has been able to build and enjoy a successful, growing practice in a fabulous new facility. In fact, he has been awarded with several Congressional Recognition Awards for his contributions to the community.

He is a passionate student of all things marketing and has lectured nationally and internationally on various dental practice management topics.

Scott is a great believer in the powers of positive thinking, focusing on the goal and then just doing it! Hence the name of his company, "justdoitdental" he co-founded with 2 other partners. He applies these concepts to all areas of his life, attributing much of his newly found opportunities and successes to them.

As a newly minted 50 year old, he just completed his first triathalon—and came in in the top 25%! Scott married his college sweetheart, Donna, in 1989 and they were blessed with three great kids. The whole family is involved in competitve swimming and enjoys skiing, golfing and traveling as a family…..still.

The Most Incredible
<u>FREE</u> Gift Ever

($633.91 Worth of Pure MoneyMaking Information)

Dan Kennedy & Bill Glazer are offering an incredible opportunity for you to see WHY <u>Glazer-Kennedy Insider's Circle</u>™ is known as "<u>THE PLACE</u>" where entrepreneurs seeking <u>FAST and Dramatic Growth and greater Control, Independence, and Security come together</u>. Dan & Bill want to give you **$633.91 worth of pure Money-Making Information** including TWO months as an 'Elite' Gold Member of Glazer-Kennedy's Insider's Circle™. You'll receive a steady stream of MILLIONAIRE Maker Information including:

★ Glazer-Kennedy University: Series of 3 Webinars (Value = $387.00)

The 10 BIG Breakthroughs in Business Life with *"MILLIONARE Maker" Dan Kennedy*
- HOW <u>Any</u> Entrepreneur or Sales Professional can Multiply INCOME by 10X
- **HOW to Avoid Once and for All being an *"Advertising Victim"***
- The "*<u>Hidden Goldmine</u>*" in Everyone's Business and HOW to Capitalize on it
- **The BIGGEST MISTAKE most Entrepreneurs make in their Marketing**
- And the <u>BIGGEEE</u>…Getting Customers Seeking You Out.

The ESSENTIALS to Writing Million Dollar Ads & Sales Letters BOTH Online & Offline
with *Bill Glazer*
- How to INCREASE the Selling Power of <u>All</u> Your Advertising with the <u>13 "Must Have" Direct Response Principles</u>
- **Key Elements that Determine the Success of Your Website**
- How to Craft a Headline the Grabs the Reader's Attention
- **HOW to Create an Irresistible Offer that Melts Away <u>Any</u> Resistance to Buy**
- The <u>Best</u> Ways to Create Urgency and Inspire IMMEDIATE Response
- **"*Insider Strategies*" to INCREASE Response that you <u>Must</u> be using both ONLINE & Offline**

The ESSENTIALS of Productivity & Implementation for Entrepreneurs
with *Peak Performance Coach Lee Milteer*
- How to Almost INSTANTLY be MORE Effective, Creative, Profitable, and Take MORE Time Off
- **HOW to Master the "Inner Game" of Personal Peak Productivity**
- How to Get MORE Done in Less Time
- **HOW to Get Others to Work On <u>Your</u> Schedule**
- How to Create Clear Goals for SUCESSFUL Implementation
- **And Finally the <u>BIGGEE</u>…HOW to Stop Talking and Planning Your Dreams and Start Implementing them into Reality**

★ 'Elite' Gold Insider's Circle Membership (Two Months Value = $119.94):

- TWO Issues of *The NO B.S. Marketing Letter:*

Each issue is at least 24 pages – usually MORE – Overflowing with **the latest Marketing & MoneyMaking Strategies**. Current members refer to it as <u>a day-long intense seminar in print</u>, arriving by first class mail every month. There are ALWAYS terrific examples of ***"What's-Working-NOW"* Strategies**, timely Marketing news, trends, ongoing teaching of <u>Dan Kennedy's Most IMPORTANT Strategies</u>… and MORE. As soon as it arrives in your mailbox you'll want to find a quiet place, grab a highlighter, and devour every word.

- Two CDs Of The **EXCLUSIVE GOLD AUDIO INTERVIEWS**

EXCLUSIVE interviews with <u>successful users of direct response advertising, leading experts and entrepreneurs in direct marketing, and famous business authors and speakers</u>. Use them to turn commuting hours into **"POWER Thinking" Hours.**

★ **The New Member No B.S. Income Explosion Guide & CD** (Value = $29.97)
This resource is <u>especially designed for NEW MEMBERS</u> to show them HOW they can join the thousands of Established Members **creating exciting sales and PROFIT growth** in their Business, Practices, or Sales Careers & Greater SUCCESS in their Business lives.

★ **Income Explosion FAST START Tele-Seminar with Dan Kennedy, Bill Glazer, and Lee Milteer** (Value = $97.00)
Attend from the privacy and comfort of your home or office…hear a DYNAMIC discussion <u>of Key Advertising, Marketing, Promotion, Entrepreneurial & Phenomenon strategies</u>, PLUS answers to the most Frequently Asked Questions about these Strategies

★ **You'll also get these Exclusive "Members Only" Perks:**

- **Special FREE Gold Member CALL-IN TIMES:** Several times a year, Dan & I schedule Gold-Member ONLY Call-In times
- **Gold Member RESTRICTED ACCESS WEBSITE**: Past issues of the *NO B.S. Marketing Letter*, articles, special news, etc.
- **Continually Updated MILLION DOLLAR RESOURCE DIRECTORY** with Contacts and Resources Dan & his clients use.

*There is a one-time charge of $19.95 in North America or $39.95 International to cover postage. After your 2-Month FREE test-drive, you will automatically continue at the <u>lowest</u> Gold Member price of $59.97 per month ($69.97 outside North America). Should you decide to cancel your membership, you can do so at any time by calling Glazer-Kennedy Insider's Circle™ at 410-825-8600 or faxing a cancellation note to 410-825-3301 (Monday through Friday 9am – 5pm). Remember, your credit card will NOT be charged the low monthly membership fee until the beginning of the third month, which means you will receive 2 full issues to read, test, and **profit from all of the powerful techniques and strategies you get from being an Insider's Circle Gold Member.** And of course, it's impossible for you to lose, because if you don't absolutely LOVE everything you get, you can simply cancel your membership after the second free issue and never get billed a single penny for membership.

***EMAIL REQUIRED IN ORDER TO NOTIFY YOU ABOUT THE
GLAZER-KENNEDY UNIVERSITY WEBINARS AND FAST START TELESEMINAR***

Name _____ Business Name _____

Address _____

City _____ State _____ Postal Code _____Country_____

Phone _____ Fax_____

e-mail* _____

Credit Card Instructions to Cover $19.95 Postage ($39.95 International)

Credit Card: _____Visa _____MasterCard _____ American Express _____ Discover

Credit Card Number _____ Exp. Date _____

Signature _____ Date _____

Providing this information constitutes your permission for Glazer-Kennedy Insider's Circle™ to contact you regarding related information via mail, e-mail, fax, and phone.

FAX BACK TO 410-825-3301
Or mail to: 401 Jefferson Ave., Towson, MD 21286
www.PeakPerformersGift.com

How can you use this book?

MOTIVATE

EDUCATE

THANK

INSPIRE

PROMOTE

CONNECT

Why have a custom version of *Secrets of Peak Performers Volume II*?

- Build personal bonds with customers, prospects, employees, donors, and key constituencies

- Develop a long-lasting reminder of your event, milestone, or celebration

- Provide a keepsake that inspires change in behavior and change in lives

- Deliver the ultimate "thank you" gift that remains on coffee tables and bookshelves

- Generate the "wow" factor

Books are thoughtful gifts that provide a genuine sentiment that other promotional items cannot express. They promote employee discussions and interaction, reinforce an event's meaning or location, and they make a lasting impression. Use your book to say "Thank You" and show people that you care.

Secrets of Peak Performers Volume II is available in bulk quantities and in customized versions at special discounts for corporate, institutional, and educational purposes. To learn more please contact our Special Sales team at: **1.866.775.1696** • **sales@advantageww.com** • **wwwAdvantageSpecialSales.com**

Printed in the USA
CPSIA information can be obtained
at www.ICGtesting.com
JSHW012037140824
68134JS00033B/3110